Judged Innocent

By Mark Rowan

© Copyright 2021 by Mark Rowan

All rights reserved. No part of this publication may be reproduced, stored in a retrieval system, or transmitted in any form or by any means—electronic, mechanical, photocopy, recording, or any other—except for brief quotations in printed reviews, without the express written permission from the author. Reach him at:

markrowanccc@gmail.com
www.hubonthestrand.co.uk

ISBN: 978-1-7398903-0-8

Table of Contents

Dedication 7
Acknowledgements 9
Forewords 11
Introduction 13
Chapter 1: Early Life 17
Chapter 2: "You'll Never Amount to Anything" ... 25
Chapter 3: Numb, Confused, and Out of Control ... 29
Chapter 4: Sent Away 33
Chapter 5: Rivendell Children's Home 37
Chapter 6: Castle Howard 41
Chapter 7: Trying it out at Home Again 47
Chapter 8: John and James, Partners in Crime ... 51
Chapter 9: Prison with my Pals 55
Chapter 10: Slop Out! 57
Chapter 11: Exercise, Exercise! 61
Chapter 12: Life at Armley 65
Chapter 13: Judgement Day! 69
Chapter 14: Beginnings of Addiction 73
Chapter 15: Smuggling Drugs into Armley 77
Chapter 16: Sent to Ever Thorpe 81
Chapter 17: 28 Days of Solitary 85
Chapter 18: Full-Scale Riot 89

Chapter 19: Life of Crime and Addiction	93
Chapter 20: Giving a Go at Work	99
Chapter 21: Arrested, Charged…and Released!	103
Chapter 22: Party!	107
Chapter 23: Heroin and Drug Dens	111
Chapter 24: Jenny and Roxanne	115
Chapter 25: The Never-ending Cycle	119
Chapter 26: Finding Heroin	123
Chapter 27: Shipped to Ranby	127
Chapter 28: Out of Prison and Out of Control	131
Chapter 29: Back to Prison	137
Chapter 30: Another Crime Spree	141
Chapter 31: Heading to the Therapy Unit	145
Chapter 32: Discovering the Drug-Free Me	149
Chapter 33: Matty, the God Squad	151
Chapter 34: Coming to Know Jesus Christ	155
Chapter 35: My New Identity in Christ	159
Chapter 36: Leading Others to Christ	163
Chapter 37: New Life, New Friends, Drug-Free	167
Chapter 38: Sensing God's Presence	171
Chapter 39: A Doorkeeper in the House of God	175
Chapter 40: Restored Family Relationships	177
Chapter 41: Speaking into Precious Lives	179
Chapter 42: Miracles in the Mission Field	181
Chapter 43: Meeting My Wife	185

Chapter 44: "Sylvester the Cat"
    Proposes to Andrea   189
  Chapter 45: Our Wedding   193
Chapter 46: Miracles at Weston-Super-Mare   195
Chapter 47: Growing our Family   199
Chapter 48: The Beginnings of Full-Time Ministry   203
Chapter 49: Pastoring My First Church   207
Chapter 50: My Own Miraculous Healing   211
Chapter 51: Miracles in Barnstaple   215
Chapter 52: A God-Given Vision for a
    New Community   217
Chapter 53: Jesus Can Change Your Life Today   221

Dedication

I wrote this book in memory of my brother, Wayne Rowan, who sadly took his own life in his prison cell at HMP Armley Prison Leeds on Christmas Eve 2001.

You'll never be forgotten. Love you always, Mark.

Acknowledgements

My sincere thanks to my friends and family for their constant encouragement and support during the writing of this book.

Thanks also to you, the readers, who encouraged me to extend my first book into this new edition.

Thanks also to Sue Jewitt for the cover design, to Donna Ferrier for the editing, and to Simon Ellery for photography.

Forewords

Mark is one of the men who is proof of the power of the Almighty Saviour to save. I have had the privilege of being a prison chaplain for forty years and am now retired. Watching Mark grow in the ministry has been one of the rewards of my many years of ministry.

—Rev Bill Hill

As the little saying goes, "Every face tells a story," and Mark's story is definitely worth reading.

Having known him for over twenty years and following closely his wonderful testimony of grace and God's call upon his life, I can 100 percent recommend this excellent book that will certainly bless and encourage every reader.

—John Partington

Introduction

Jeremiah 1:5 tells us that even as he was being formed in his mother's womb, God knew his name and planned him for a purpose. Friends, before you start reading this book, I want you to know that you were planned for a purpose. God knows your name. There's purpose and destiny on your life. God calls you his masterpiece. You are completely unique, and he has created you to do great things in this life.

For half my life, I lived on this planet, disconnected from God, feeling as though I had no purpose. At times I found myself questioning if there was any meaning to life at all, until I found God, connected with others, and discovered my purpose.

This is my personal story of how one encounter with God radically transformed my life forever.

As you read this book, I pray you will see that believing in Jesus Christ really does set you free.

Through many dangers, toils, and snares,
I have already come;
'Tis grace hath brought me safe thus far,
And grace will lead me home.

—John Newton

Chapter 1

Early Life

The year 1970 was a great year in the UK. It was the year the Concorde, our first supersonic jumbo jet, went into service.

It was also the year of our first isle of white rock festival and the year Apollo 13 landed on the moon for the third time. Another amazing thing happened somewhere in Dewsbury District Hospital: I took my first breath and got my first glimpse of the world.

People who have known me for many years are amazed that I am still alive to tell this story. We all have a book in us and a story to tell. I just wrote mine down.

I have lived a crazy life of guns, gangs, drugs, and violence. I was lost, broken, and needed help. I found that help. Jesus rocked my world and changed everything in it for the good. He can do the same for you today. So, sit back, fasten your seat belts, and enjoy the ride. This is my story.

I was four years old in 1974, and my family, consisting of my two brothers, my parents, and myself, lived in a small, terraced house in a place called Heckmondwike. We were brought up as hunters. My dad always had ferrets and hunting dogs, and we were putting out traps and skinning rabbits as soon as we could walk.

My dad had a bit of a reputation as a fearless fighter. Unfortunately, he also loved to drink. He often came home drunk. If he didn't make it home, the police would knock and let my mum know where he was. We had no phones in our home back then. The nearest phone was a phone box that everyone shared a few streets away.

Sometimes my dad never came home at all, and we would be taken to visit him in some large scary building that looked like the hammered house of horrors.

One of my earliest childhood memories was visiting my dad in a high-security prison. I remember the overpowering smell of urine and cigarette smoke and seeing the bars on the windows and the razor wire on top of the high walls. I also remember seeing the guard dogs patrolling the perimeter inside those walls.

I remember being squashed in a room with lots of people waiting to visit their family members. I wondered why I was being searched since I was only nine years old.

Suddenly the door opened, and an officer shouted my dad's last name at the top of his voice: "Rowan Visit!"

My grandma stood up, held our hands, and walked my brother, Danny, and me through the hall. There were rows and rows of tables full of men waiting for their visits. For a moment, I couldn't find my dad, but then I saw him sitting and waiting for us at the table.

I wondered what he had done and why he was there. We never asked him, and he never told us, but he was my dad, and I wanted to be just like him.

We never had much at home. When Dad was in prison, Mum would walk us miles to our gran's house to get breakfast or dinner. My gran was a legend and always smothered us with love, chocolate, and smoky kisses. She kept her teeth in a glass next to her still-burning cigarette in the ashtray, which was a bit scary when I was a kid, but I got used to it.

When Dad was finally released from prison, he came home steaming drunk. I remember him teaching me how to box. He showed me how to make a fist, and then he would punch his hands and shout, "Left! Right! Right jab! Right! Left!"

I've still only seen my dad a few times throughout my life, but the one memory that sticks out was when he came home drunk and gave the only food we had left to the dogs. I still remember my mum saying, "Billy, that's all we have left, the tin the pie is in." He threw the pie at my mum because she protested about it. I remember its sharp edges sticking in the door near me as I was in her arms.

Mum soon left my dad, taking us with her, and we moved about five miles away to a place called Hightown in Cleckheaton, a rough council estate that lived up to its well-known reputation. But I still felt so excited and safe when we moved into our three-bed council house on Fifth Avenue East. My brothers and I had lots of space, and we had our own bedrooms. Little did we know it would quickly become overcrowded.

I remember the local window cleaner washing our windows for the first time. He was very friendly with my mum. After a few more visits, he started coming in the house to chat with Mum. A few weeks later we were visiting the window cleaner's house. He was a single dad with three boys. Meeting the boys felt a bit awkward. I didn't understand why we were visiting them.

But after a few months, Allan, the window cleaner, and his three sons moved into our house with us. Eight of us were now living in a three-bed council house, so bunk beds were put in the bedrooms.

Allan, my new stepfather, also liked to drink and spent a lot of time at the local bars and pubs. Often my mum would join him in the evenings. The partying didn't stop after last orders at the pub. A large crowd of strangers would often be invited back to the house to carry on drinking from the bar, which was built into a corner of the living room, into the early hours of the morning. This usually resulted in strangers being sick in the bathroom.

The noise of laughter and singing filled the air, along with the thick smell of cigarettes and alcohol. But sometimes the sound of arguments and fights would suddenly rise above the music, and drunk strangers would wander into our bedrooms, looking for the toilet.

When everyone had gone home, new arguments would always start, which usually ended with my mum being beaten up again. Many times she had black eyes or a busted nose. Once she was thrown down the stairs, resulting in a broken arm. As kids, we would just listen and hope it would stop, but it never did. I felt powerless. I wanted to grow up quick so I could protect my mum from the beatings.

We were always told to tell anyone who asked about the bruises that she fell down the stairs. We knew it was lying, but we did as we were told because we were afraid of getting beaten too. It seemed my younger brother, Wayne, and I were good target practice. We would often get beaten with the buckle of a leather belt, or a fist. Sometimes, with our hands on our heads, we had to stand in a corner and face the wall for punishments for small things.

We were far from being little angels. We would do anything we could to get out of the house, and once we were out, we would cause trouble in the streets. We would form small gangs and smash windows of factories from the trainlines and wait to be chased. We would light fires and throw fireworks (bangers) at one another. I realise now that this was a dumb and dangerous thing to do, yet this was normal for a kid my age on the estate. We often balanced glass bottles on the door handles of people we didn't like, and then we'd knock on the door and run away. We would carve wood into the shape of gun and pretend we were in the army. We made the sounds of shots as we "fired" at each other and played dead once we had been shot. I felt free and safe outside. I never wanted to go home.

One Christmas I got a second-hand BMX. I spent hours outside each day playing on that BMX, learning all kinds of cool tricks. The local kids my age began calling me "superkid." Soon small pockets of people would come knocking on the door, asking if superkid was in.

Superkid seemed to be my nickname for a while. I didn't get much attention at home, so I revelled in my role as superkid, risking life and limb to entertain others who didn't have the balls to try the crazy stunts I was doing. I would carry my bike up the slide in the park and there was a steep ramp at the bottom. Well, you can guess the rest. I would put builders planks up against goal posts and go for the jump.

One evening we lit a fire in the park, as bored kids on the estate usually did, and we threw a metal sheet over the fire. Whilst a few attempts at running and jumping through the fire were successful, on the third attempt, my rubber-soled shoes hit the scorching metal. It was like an ice rink. I slipped and landed on my backside but, to the sound of cheers, I managed to escape from the fire. Embarrassingly I looked like a baboon as my burnt, raw, blistered backside was hanging out either side of my jeans for the world to see. It was all in the name of fun, of course, and to keep my ridiculous superkid reputation intact.

Although I had seen the effects of drinking and how it changed a person's personality, curiosity got the better of me and I decided to see for myself what drinks tasted like. Like clockwork, my mum and stepdad would be out at the pub, and I would go to the bar in the corner of the living room and try the whiskey, rum, and vodka. It was like drinking firewater, but I liked the taste and was careful how much I drank. I always wanted more but didn't want to get caught, so I always topped them back up with water. I think the only reason I never got caught was by the time anyone had a drink from the bar, they were already drunk and didn't notice.

I also went through a time of experimenting with anything I could get my hands on to escape reality. I felt as though I was on my own personal mission of self-destruction. Soon I started sniffing solvents to get high and hallucinate. It started with sniffing gas. I would press the nozzle against my teeth and inhale. I usually lost all sense of reality and often came round in different places, not knowing how I got there. I didn't feel loved and didn't seem to care whether I lived or died. Soon other substances became a regular part of my day. Glue and petrol were often on my daily menu, anything to escape the present reality.

I also seemed to have an obsession with war and collected war magazines and memorabilia. I started a knife collection. My first knife was a Ghurkha, and my second was a Chinese knife. I collected old war medals and would spend considerable time down the fields in the old air raid bunkers, digging to find bones and bullets left by soldiers. I never found anything, but I always dreamed of becoming a soldier and going to war to fight for my country.

Looking back over my life, I must have seemed like such a weird kid. Most kids my age had a cat or a dog, whereas my pets were usually ferrets and polecats that would often follow me up and down the street. I also had a pet fox. Kids my age would buy sweets from the shop, but whenever I had the chance, I would buy a block of cheese and a tin of cold sprats and spent most of my time trapping birds. Once I caught the birds, I would dissect them with my pocketknife to feed to my polecats and ferrets.

Chapter 2

"You'll Never Amount to Anything"

The shouting and the violence at home seemed to escalate. We went from peace to chaos in a moment. I was frustrated, confused, and full of anger. I wanted to make it stop, but I knew I didn't have the strength. I was just a kid, and my stepdad was a man. When I was eleven years old, I stole an axe from the garden shed and started chopping up the local park in frustration and anger. The local police were called, and I was arrested, cautioned, and taken home.

I was bored, empty, and lost. I was often told I would never amount to anything, and even though I believed it, I often wondered, *What if I had a purpose and there really was more to life than I had experienced?* Little did I know that God had a purpose for my life, and he was always trying to get my attention to follow him and step into that purpose.

I hardly ever went to school. Even when I did go, I always struggled to concentrate. I'd spend most of my time daydreaming, looking out of the window. My clothes were always too big, so I would grow into them, and they would last longer. I was always bullied at school, though I fought back on many occasions, which resulted in a few trips to the headmaster's office. He put me over his knees and hit me with the slipper. A couple of times I got caned on my hands, with bamboo. This was an acceptable form of punishment back then, and parents agreed to it.

Each morning our headmaster would make us sit with our arms and legs crossed, in neat, straight lines on the floor. Once we were all in place and the hall was full, the headmaster would say, "Good morning," and play his acoustic guitar while we sang along to songs like "Morning Has Broken." One morning while he was playing his guitar there was noise and shuffling. He stood up and had a compete meltdown. To our surprise he smashed his guitar on the stage right in front of us, which I thought was cool at the time. But apart from that, I thought school was boring.

When I set off to school in the mornings, I always told people I was taking a secret shortcut and head to the fields to look for adventure. I would spend the day alone sniffing glue and getting high in abandoned warehouses. I soon realised I needed money for more glue to stay high, so I began to plan how I could get glue. I was bunking off school one day when I saw someone leaving their home to go out. Once they had gotten into their car and drove away, I knocked on the door and looked through the window. There was no answer, so I smashed the window, climbed inside the house, and stole some small change and food.

I know I should have felt guilty. I knew this was wrong and I could have been in serious trouble. But instead, I realised I had found a way to get money so I could get high and food to eat. I was always hungry. Every time I would run away from the chaotic arguments and beatings at home, I never had anywhere to go. I just wanted to get as far away as I could to start a new life. In my heart I believed it was possible, but I was a scared, lost kid. I would put on an extra jumper and a big coat, then leave to wander the fields and streets for hours and hours.

Chapter 3

Numb, Confused, and Out of Control

When the sun went down and it got dark, I knew people might be looking for me, so when I saw car lights approaching, I would jump behind a bush or over a wall until the car had passed by. It was freezing cold, and I didn't have any blankets, so I usually tried to go to sleep in the sheds of empty houses. I didn't sleep much at all, though, as I had to shoo away the occasional rat that wanted to share my shed. Even though I was scared, I was determined never to go back home.

Eventually the police would catch me following the milkman around in the morning, drinking the bottles of milk he had just delivered to various houses. They would give me a good telling off and take me back home, always to smiles, hugs, and cuddles until the police left. Then out would come the belt for a beating, and then I would be standing up with my hands behind my head and my nose against the wall.

I felt numb, confused, and out of control. I hadn't thought about the people I was hurting or about the consequences of my actions. I began to get arrested on a regular basis for petty crimes, and eventually I had to go to court and stand before the judges. I was always rude and swore at them, as I soon began to realise that I disliked anyone in authority. I also didn't have much fear or remorse for the crimes I had committed. I just felt numb and disconnected.

On this occasion in court, the judge gave me a supervision order and a social worker to be accountable to; I never understood what a social worker was, and I never listened to anything he had to say. Everything went in one ear and out the other. My family made it clear that having a social worker visit the house was bad news, but I always tried to avoid his visits anyway.

One night my mum had gone to the pub with her drinking friends. My oldest stepbrother was looking after us, and we watched a film called "Warriors," about a New York street gang, that inspired me to form my first gang. In the movie, the gang members painted their jackets with their signs and fought other gangs on the streets with bare knuckles, chains, and knives. The next day I smeared a red skull and crossbones on the back of my jacket and went out to recruit members to join my gang. I often carried my butterfly flick knife from my knife collection in case we had trouble.

Our small gang grew to three or four. It wasn't huge. We were just kids rebelling. Our main pastime was stealing bottles of cider or spirits; lacing them with Anadins, Paracetamols, sleeping pills, or any other pills we could swallow; and drinking it all. Our meetings would always end in a fight or another arrest. One of the gang members showed me his dad's shed where a huge stash of adult pornography was hidden. We both looked through it, fascinated with the images. We didn't understand it, but we thought we were cool. In reality, we were being pulled further away from God and didn't even know it.

The gang didn't last too long, and we all moved onto other things. I had made many enemies. I still carried my knife and never went anywhere without it. This was the 1980s, when there were many skinheads and punk rock bands, so I often shaved my head and wore torn union jack T-shirts with anarchist slogans on them; torn, slashed skin-tight bleached jeans; and my knee-high Doc Martin boots and red braces. My ears and my nose were full of piercings, and I was loud and foul mouthed.

Chapter 4
Sent Away

Once, out of the blue, my real dad visited me. He was drunk, and I sat next to him on the sofa, enjoying every moment, watching my stepfather shift around uncomfortably in his chair. I wondered what would happen if I told my real father how much he beat us up. Soon my real dad went off to visit some old hunting mates for a drink on the estate, and my mum and stepdad went out to the pub for a few drinks.

We were all at home when a few hours later, Shane, the eldest stepbrother, who was looking after us, ran into our bedroom and shouted, "Quick! Come and look at what was just left in the kitchen!" My real dad had returned drunk with a semi-automatic rifle and asked him to hide it in the food cupboard. until he came back. Fascinated with war, I thought this was so coolest thing that had ever happened to me, and everything in me so desperately wanted to pull the trigger. I laid in bed, trying to pluck up the courage to go down and fire the gun, but thankfully I fell asleep.

As soon as I woke up, I ran down the stairs to check the cupboard for the gun. It was gone.

And no one ever spoke of it again.

Allan would often come home from his window cleaning rounds and leave his money belt hanging in the hall. Sometimes I would steal some of the money as revenge for beating up Mum and use it get high or drunk. Sometimes if the fair was in town, I would give the money to people wanting to go on the rides. Someone always found me out, though, and took me home for a beating.

I was a low-down thief looking for places and people to steal from. Inevitably as an inexperienced juvenile, I was usually arrested and given bail with a date to attend court again. In 1983, when I was thirteen, I was charged with two counts of burglary, and the court gave me a thirty-six-hour attendance centre at a building for youth offenders in Dewsbury. Attendance centre was supposed to be a short sharp shock for young offenders.

On my first day there, I was nervous about what this short sharp shock would be. I thought I was going to be strapped to a chair and given electric short sharp shocks to sort out my behaviour and my head. But thankfully that was not the case. In fact, I met lots of kids just like me, young, confused, and angry. Big ex-Army guys were marching us around, shouting at us, and commanding us to do press ups and sit ups. We also had to climb old, smelly, sweaty ropes. I loved it, even though I knew it was supposed to be punishment for my behaviour. I stayed out of trouble for the time being, attended all the sessions, and I quite enjoyed my short sharp shock experience, which shows just how messed up my head was.

Home life was still the same, though, and wasn't getting any better. My behaviour wasn't helping the situation. One night everything was about to change when my mum and stepdad came home drunk from the pub. We all heard an almighty argument downstairs about me and my behaviour. It was late, and the argument woke the whole house up. I heard my stepfather give my mother a final ultimatum: "Either he goes, or I am leaving and taking my boys with me." I knew this was serious and I was scared. Those words were embedded and burnt into my heart for many years to come.

The next day, to my surprise, my social worker picked me up and placed me into the care of the local authorities. They put me in my first children's home.

Chapter 5

Rivendell Children's Home

Rivendell Children's home was dark, depressing, and full of abandoned kids just like me. I remember laying on my bed the first night absolutely gutted knowing the rest of my family was safe at home. The children's home was full of young punks sporting boots, mohawks, chains, and piercings. It was the era of punk rock and the Sex Pistols, the band of the moment.

With all the anger in me, I felt like a pressure cooker ready to blow. I began to sniff glue with the other punks. We would often sit on the bench at the bus station and hallucinate as we watched all the people rush around. Looking back now, I've realised that those passing by us saw us as just a bunch of lost thugs looking for trouble. This was true, but we were just a bunch of kids who wanted to be loved.

The children's home was a strange, tense environment. Punk music would blast out of residents' bedrooms, and most of the girls and lads were sleeping with each other. Some residents attempted suicide;

some were self-harming daily. One of the lads would always cut himself with knives and razor blades and boast of his latest cuts.

One day I got into a fight. The staff jumped on me to restrain me. I fought with them on the floor, and they dragged me into a bedroom and locked me in. In a rage of anger, I picked up a set of draws, threw them through the ground floor bedroom window, jumped out, and ran back to continue the fight. I was told I would have to be moved if my behaviour continued.

All was calm for a little while. A week later a member of staff left her handbag in the kitchen. Someone distracted her while another resident stole the car keys, and a few of us went for a joy ride. None of us had ever driven anything before we set off screeching down the road in first gear, screaming and shouting like a bunch of lunatics and smashing into the railings and walls. Our adrenaline was pumping as we flew around the local town centre at high speed.

It wasn't long before the police were called, and they began chasing us. It was all over in a flash. The car was totalled, and we nearly killed ourselves, but none of us really cared.

This incident brought me once again before the court judges. As usual I was rude to the judge as I had no respect for him. I didn't care for the situation either, even though my life was in his hands. The judge decided I was to be moved to a place far away called Castle Howard. I had no idea where that was.

My social worker put me in the car, and we began the longest journey ever. It took five hours to get there. I had never been so far away from home. It felt like a million miles away from anywhere I knew. After the long drive, we finally turned off the motorway and followed the signs for Castle Howard. Turns out it was deep in the middle of the woods, somewhere near York and Molton.

Chapter 6

Castle Howard

Castle Howard was comprised of three units, two boys' houses and a girls' unit, round a huge paddock surrounded by woods. It was a remand unit for troubled juveniles. The courts from Grimsby, Scunthorpe and Immingham sent kids there as they awaited their court dates. It was a massive place and full of varied colourful characters. It was strange meeting a whole new bunch of people again and trying to settle into a new place. I didn't know it yet, but this was going to be home for the next few years.

I soon found my feet and a little crew to hang with. Friendships were difficult for me over the next few years as everyone else was on remand and I was on a care order, so I saw many people constantly come and go. When the others were taken to court on their appointed court dates, I never saw them again unless they were remanded there again for other crimes they committed in the future. Sometimes I would see an old face drop by again on remand.

I started to realise everyone was getting lots of mail and visits from their family. I was jealous and envious because I had none, but eventually I became numb to it and focused on physical exercise, pounding the punching bag at the gym, trying to find some relief from the anger inside. I was driven with a desire for revenge.

Mr Tate, one of the house staff, became my good friend to the end. He would hold back all the leftover fruit and vegetables for me to eat. He would constantly put extra weights on my bench press and scream, "More! More, Mark, more!" We would often have football matches with other places from outside. I was always on the team even though I was absolutely rubbish at football. I was the chopper; my soul purpose was taking people out of the game. Mr Tate would whisper in my ear who my new target was and say, "Take them out. Chop them down. Go, go, go." I loved him for it and did as I was told. I was usually sent off as quickly as I came on but always managed to take out a good player on the other team first.

Our physical training with Mr Tate was always fun and complete carnage. He would always get us to play murder ball, which always seemed to sort the men from the boys. Murder ball consisted of two teams, one team at one side of the indoor hall, and another at the other end, with one big medicine ball in the middle. The name of the game was to charge the ball and get it to the other side at any cost. It always ended in a big pile up with black eyes and bust noses, but we all loved it. It was always a good time to give someone I didn't like a good sneaky punch without getting told off for it.

Castle Howard also had a farm with pigs, sheep, and chickens. It was our job to feed and muck out the animals.

We loved it. It was a good laugh and gave us all something to do during the long days. I noticed the petrol cap on the land rover had no lock on it, so sometimes I would sneak down to the land rover, tie a rag on the end of a stick, dip it into the petrol tank, drop the soaked rag into a bag, and sniff the petrol with the bag over my mouth and nose, breathing the fumes in deeply until I began to hallucinate. It was my way of trying to find a momentary escape from reality. Sometimes I was caught and punished but I didn't really care if I was caught.

    I began to run away regularly with no real destination in mind, partly because for a long time, I had no idea where I really was. Once a lad and I planned to run away after head count. He was on remand from Hull. We made a run for it just before dark and followed the trainlines for a while before we came to a train station. We got on a train and hid and managed to make it all the way to Hull just before Hull City Centre. The train stopped at some traffic light, and we jumped off the train before it went into the main station.

    When we got there, he called his mates. They had a squat somewhere in an abandoned house, so we piled in through a broken window, started filling the glue bags, and sniffing together. The music was pumping. The police were called. They broke down the door and rushed in, and we were all separated. Everyone ran to different places in the city. I found myself walking the streets, hallucinating and lost.

    I was finally arrested in the early hours of the morning and taken back to Castle Howard. I was given a good telling off. I was also warned that I was on thin ice and would be moved if my behaviour didn't change.

    The unit began to take us out to the fitness centre in York to use the swimming pool. The girls from the local community would come to the steamed-up windows and watch us swim. After a couple of weeks, I began writing to them in the steam on the windows, and they wrote messages back in the same way. One day, they gave me their phone number. That was all I needed.

Every week we were given 50 pence to spend in a sweets van that came to the unit. I pretended to buy sweets from the van, but I was saving the money to run away. My plan was to save up enough money and catch a bus to York. When the day came, I hid in the bushes and waited for the bus to York. When the bus came, I got my ticket and laid down on the back seat of the bus in case the police were looking for me again.

When I arrived in York, I headed for the pool area to make the call. The girls came out to meet me, and we started drinking. The time passed quickly and soon it was dark. Two sisters I had met said they had a tent in their dad's garage, so we set up the tent in the back garden of their house. It wasn't the greatest place to hide me from their father, plus it was cold. I was armed with a knife I had taken with me.

The father was a taxi driver, and at midnight someone began to enter the tent, so I quickly pulled out my knife. It was the girls' father. I told him who I was and where I had come from. He seemed calm about it and drove me back to Castle Howard at the early hours of the morning. When we arrived at the grounds, he told me to get out of the car. Then he drove away. Half asleep and still a bit drunk, I knocked the door until a staff member finally answered. I was expecting fireworks, but he just told me to go to bed.

I never really knew where I was. I was just always running, like Forest Gump, with no real destination.

We would often get bored and get up to mischief in Castle Howard. A lot of the lads coming in on remand from other places had tattoos on their hands and faces. They had "love" and "hate" on their knuckles and teardrops on their faces. I was determined to get some tattoos. A plan was hatched to steal some ink. A few days later we had stolen some Indian ink and hid it until the staff went to the office for lunch.

I got the ink from its hiding place and a needle. I wrapped cotton round the end of the needle, dipped it into the ink pot, and began stabbing away at my fingers. I tattooed my name across all of them while they were still bleeding. I went to the bathroom and, with a pen, drew a tear on my face. Then I tried to follow the pattern as I began to tattoo my face in the mirror. I was caught in the act, full of ink and blood, and punished, but not before I managed to put a borstal dot on my right cheek a sign of rebellion and hate.

Chapter 7

Trying it out at Home Again

At the end of my second year at Castle Howard, there was a review of my care order. My mother and my social worker came to the meeting, and a date was set for me to try it out at home again. I was excited and nervous when the day finally came, and I made my way home on the train. So much had changed. The family had moved to a bigger council house. My brothers were all smiles, and I was shown which bunk I would sleep on. It all felt so awkward, and I didn't believe they really wanted me back.

The oldest stepbrother had moved out into a block of high-rise flats called Brooklyn in Cleckheaton, an area known for its wild parties and drugs. For a few days, my trial week seemed to be going OK, although I always felt disconnected and on guard. Since I had no access to a gym, I put some house bricks on each end of a sweeping brush handle and began lifting weights in the bedroom.

I felt like a gate-crashing stranger because so much had changed. Now it was my brother, Wayne, who was always being shouted at, punished, and banished to his room. I really felt for him. Having become stronger than I used to be through relentless training and gym work, I realised I was no longer afraid of my stepfather, Allan. He didn't seem the threatening, imposing figure I remembered.

The end of the week soon came around with no trouble until after closing time at the local pubs and bars. As usual lots of people came back to the house to party and drink into the early hours. My trial at home was about to come to an end when I was called into the room like a party piece to show all the strangers I was home on a trial week. I saw a sailor passionately kissing my best friend's mother on our settee, so I gave him a right hook, knocking him out on the carpet. Everyone, including me, was stunned. People were shouting and screaming at me. I had blown it again.

My granddad was beaten up and murdered that week in a local pub toilet, and this violence had brought it all to the surface. I was gutted and felt bad for what I had done.

The next morning, I was taken away for another spell in care, but I never went back to Castle Howard. This time I was put in a place called Eastmoor in Leeds. I will never forget the first day. I remember walking through the doors and being shown around. There were lads leaning against the wall, smoking their cigarettes, and trying to intimidate me.

I was finally shown my room and left alone with all my possessions. I was absolutely gutted. All I owned were my clothes. I had never felt so low. I remember wondering why I couldn't be a normal kid with a normal family and live a normal life. I was scared but knew I couldn't show any sign of weakness.

This place was different from anywhere else I had stayed. Lots of the men were from the local estates in Leeds, and they usually hung out together in gangs. Over time I had a few scrapes with people and got my face kicked in a few times, but I managed a few victories along the way and made a small group of likeminded acquaintances.

Nobody was there by choice. There was always a tense atmosphere that could kick off at any moment if someone was having a bad day. I stayed there for quite a while. The authorities arranged a second attempt to go home, and I was off.

It had been years since I lived at home, but that's where I wanted to be. I arrived at the family council house on Laverhills. Maybe this time all would finally be OK.

Everything was going so well until the weekend arrived when we heard my mum and stepfather come in drunk, as usual. Things began to get smashed. There was a loud smack followed by a scream, and I knew it was my mum being beaten and thrown down the stairs again. In years gone by, all of us would have laid in our beds, scared, listening, powerless to do anything, but now I couldn't just listen anymore. I had to protect my mum.

Adrenaline pumping, I flung open the bedroom door and charged downstairs. I ran into the room, and without hesitation, I punched him in the mouth as hard as I could, and he slid down the fireplace. All the anger and rage came out in that one blow.

My stepbrother ran down the stairs and into the room, shouting, "Stop!" and tried to grab me. In a rage I punched him, and my mother began screaming for me to get out of the house. I didn't understand. I thought she would be happy that I was finally protecting her. Although I know what I did was wrong, I didn't understand why I had to leave again. This was the last time I would be allowed to set foot into the family home.

Chapter 8

John and James, Partners in Crime

Since I wasn't welcome at home, I moved in with my gran for a while. She was a practical, down-to-earth person and solid as a rock. She always made sure my belly was full and told me to exercise. She never liked my mother and expressed it. While living with gran, I started hanging out with a local girl, and quite soon she announced she was pregnant. When she told me the baby wasn't mine, I flipped and met the alleged father to fight it out. I was heartbroken. I hit the drugs hard and moved away from the scene again.

By now I was a prolific burglar and had two partners in crime, John and James, who were brothers and lived in the area opposite the family home. I couldn't live with my gran long term and knew I had to find somewhere quickly. Through John and James, I found a place on the same street. It was awkward living so close to my family yet never speaking to them, but I could pop across the street and hang out with the brothers.

James and John were as crazy as I was. Their bedroom was decorated in the weirdest of colours, and John had a baby doll, with a knife through its head and fake blood, hanging in the window. While rolling joints and smoking bongs we blasted the street with our choice of music while we waited for the cover of darkness so we could get down to real business.

On any given evening we would be out stealing motorbikes to go pull a job somewhere. We mainly rampaged through commercial buildings, smashing doors off and looking for the keys to the safe. With our adrenalin pumping, we once stood in front of a three-foot-high safe, trying all the keys we had found in the offices. Eventually one fit and we emptied the safe and dumped the stolen bikes on our way home.

During the day the three of us would spend time hanging out, smoking joints, and doing bucket bongs until it ran out. In order to score, we had to travel to Manningham Lane in Bradford, which was the heart of the red-light district, day or night. There were often riots in and shootouts with the police in the streets. At any time of day, it was full of dodgy characters, but at night groups of prostitutes would shout for customers, like us, desperate to get our fix.

Music was always pounding from cars, and dealers were always arguing over who had seen you coming first. Most of the time our trips were successes, and we would head to the strip club in the city centre to check out our score. But one time the undercover police, who had seen me score as soon as I was a few blocks away, skidded up quickly beside me. I tried to throw drugs into the hedge, but they saw me and retrieved them.

They arrested me, took me to the police station, and charged me with possession of controlled drugs. Something inside me couldn't stop. It was as if I was determined to destroy my own life at any cost. As soon as I was released from the police station, I made my back to Manningham to get what I came for and went home.

I was spending a lot of time getting high at the brothers' house. I got to know their sister and we hooked up. Soon after, she announced we were having a baby. We were excited and I promised to be a responsible adult. But the truth was, I didn't know how to change my ways.

I used to sleep with a rifle under the bed alongside other weapons. At the time it felt the most normal thing to have under my bed because I had enemies. I would often get up early and go to the countryside to shoot rabbits and anything else that moved. I didn't really want to eat any of the stuff I shot; it was more about the chase and the kill.

One of the brothers had been sent to prison, so now it was just two of us out burgling. It was an unspoken rule that we would never come home empty handed, and we would often stay out until the morning light. Most of the time, we had no transport, so we would carry the stuff we stole, which was usually computers and office equipment, over fields and railway lines, sometimes for miles, stopping every ten minutes to give our arms a rest.

As the sun would begin to rise, we would hide our stuff in a field, camouflaging it with bushes and leaves, and come back later in the day with a potential buyer. We would always find people who wanted to buy the stuff we stole, and they would give us a list of what they wanted. So, basically, we stole to order. If computers were quite new, we would strip out the serial numbers and give them new ones before selling them on the shelves in a friend's computer shop. We would always spend the money on clothes and drugs, shooting up and snorting until the money ran out.

Chapter 9

Prison with my Pals

Sometimes, the police would smash the door in the early hours of the morning, arrest us, charge us, and sling us in the cells as we awaited our court appearance. Both of the brothers had been to prison before and had done plenty of bird, but I hadn't. They knew what was coming. We were escorted to the courts in a van and put in a holding cell.

Eventually, after many hours, our names would be called, and we were handcuffed and taking up the stairs into the courtroom to face the judges. We stood side by side and gave our names. After the charges were read, we stood to receive our punishment. The first brother was denied bail and sent to prison. The second brother was also jailed, but for some reason they gave me bail.

At this point, any normal person would have been relieved to possibly go free, but I went berserk, shouting and verbally abusing the judge, demanding I to go to prison with my pals. I can still remember the look on the face of my solicitor, who had put up a brave fight for me to receive bail. The judge was shocked as well at my carefully chosen words, which had the desired effect, and I too was remanded into custody. Everyone thought I was crazy, but I saw my actions as loyal. I was going to stand with them no matter what. I soon learned, however, there was no real honour or loyalty in the underworld.

So down to the cells I went. After about five hours of waiting around, the brothers, the other prisoners, and I were all cuffed together, bundled into a meat van, and driven to HMP Armley. The van stopped at various places and picked up more prisoners. We laughed and joked, but I could sense an uneasiness in the air.

After a while, someone said, "Here we are, boys." As we looked out the van window upon the hill in the distance, we saw a huge black castle with massive gates around twenty feet tall, full of bars and razor wire everywhere. It looked like something out of a horror movie.

As we approached the gates, they were opened and officers with snarling, barking dogs greeted us. The officers lined us up and pointed for us to get in the tunnel, which led to the reception area. The place stank with an overpowering smell of urine and cigarette smoke. It was a messed-up and dirty scene.

Chapter 10

Slop Out!

One by one we stood on a yellow line, gave our names, and were uncuffed and sent into another packed room. It was full of people from up and down the country who had been remanded or just sentenced. I sat and listened to them. Some had received life sentences for murder, while others were there for burglary or stealing cars. Some had been there for eight years, and others just a few months. Some were being threatened from disputes from the streets. Others were smoking joints. While someone kept a watch for the officers, I was nervous and uncomfortable for the first time, but I was determined not to show any sign of weakness and become an easy target.

After a couple of hours, my name was called, and I had to follow the yellow line on the floor, which led to a table with a box on it, and strip naked in front of two officers. I had to chuck my clothes in the box, put my hands behind my head, and squat to the floor. Then I had to open my mouth so the guard could check for drugs. I was free to carry on, following the yellow line, still naked, to the freezing packed showers. After the showers I was handed a very dodgy smelly prison uniform consisting of a very creased bright green shirt with seventies collars and dark brown flared denim jeans.

I am sure the prison uniform was designed to make us feel worse. I know we were not dressing for the catwalk, but it was grim. It was obvious the underpants hadn't been washed from the previous prisoners. If we wanted a good kit, we had to give other prisoners who worked in that area weed or tobacco. Eventually we were given our bedrolls, blankets, and sheets and told to follow the officers to the wings.

As we turned the corner into the main prison, I noticed the smell and the stink of urine was even stronger. I saw a cockroach running ahead of me on the floor and several others on the ground that other people had already killed. When the other prisoners saw the new arrivals coming, they would try to intimidate us. They would blow kisses, whistle, rattle their cups on their prison bars, and kick their doors while shouting, "New blood! Watch out; new blood! I will wait for you in the showers! Welcome to hell! Welcome to your worst nightmare, new bloods!" Each wing had three floors with about a hundred people each. I was given a card with a number on it and told to wait outside the door. I found my cell.

When the guard unlocked the door and put me inside, nothing could have prepared me for the scene that greeted me. The stink was unbearable. There was a bunkbed and a chair, and, in the corner, a bucket filled to the top with wee and no lid, and number two floating in it. Cigarette butts were all over the floor and pornography covered some of the walls from floor to ceiling, This I was to discover was the norm.

In the spaces where there was no porn, prisoners had scratched their names and sentences on the back of the thick, dirty, rusty door. There were stains on the walls and the ceiling where trays of unwanted prison food had been thrown in anger, and other suspect marks, which were obviously people picking their nose. At the back of the tiny, cramped cell were too very small, arched windows covered by bars just wide enough to get my hand through.

I introduced myself to my cellmate, and we had the usual exchange of questions: "What you in for?" "Where you from?" "How long you in for?" At that moment I didn't realise I would go through these questions many times over the years. We weighed each other up for a few moments for signs of weaknesses since it was obvious I didn't know the score or the routine.

I confessed it was my first time and bombarded my cellmate with an avalanche of questions. As we were chatting, someone began to bang on the ceiling from above. I realised I was on the second of three floors. My name was being shouted above me. I immediately recognised the voice. It was one of the brothers yelling, "Mark, come to your bars!" Jumping to the window, I saw a rollup on a piece of string dangling in front of me outside the bars. Laughing, I reached through the bars to retrieve it. This was my first-ever line. I tugged the line to signal I had the goods, and up it went.

"See you tomorrow on exercise!"

"OK, later, mate."

My cellmate began to tear his bottom bedsheet into thin strips and tie them together as he had to get something from the boys in the cell underneath us. When it was long enough, a bar of prison soap or some kind of weight would be attached to the bottom of the line. Then it would be lowered out the window to the cell below to retrieve goods or pass stuff down. People in other cells would try to steal what was on the lines as they were being thrown left and right. Small prison-issue metal mirrors would be held out of the bars to keep an eye on the goods every step of the way. If anyone did steal the stuff, it would be dealt with, with violence, on the exercise yard the next day.

The next morning was an eye opener. The door opened, and a waft of breakfast porridge and urine filled the air. It was slop out. It was as though I had stepped out of my cell and into hell. I found about fifty men all queuing up with buckets full of urine and turds, and boy it stank. There were small spills on the floor. I spotted people I knew and gave them a shout. Everyone was shouting and trying to hustle for stuff they needed: rizlas, matches, tobacco, as well as porn mags and newspapers. Holding my breath and nearly puking, I emptied the bucket down the sluice. Cockroaches lay dead and squashed on the floor around me.

The slop-out area is usually where many fights were had. Buckets accidently spilling and splashing one another could kick off in a second. Being on the middle floor, I could see the people doing the same on the first floor that we were on our floor. Separating us was a wire mesh as if it were a roof. People were sometimes thrown over the rails in fights from the floor above, so the mesh served as a hardcore safety net. One time a prison officer was thrown over.

I could see a prison officer on the floor below, and I was tempted to throw the contents of my bucket over him, which also occasionally happened. An officer would shout at the top of his voice, "Slop out is finished! Get in your cells now! Rowan, get in your cell now! You're just like your father!" Obviously, my dad was known inside and out.

Chapter 11

Exercise, Exercise!

Armley was a remand prison. We were locked in our cells twenty-three hours a day with one hour exercise, though if it rained it was called off. The days were very long and very boring. Soon after breakfast, the door would be unlocked to the sound of officers shouting, "Exercise! Exercise!" Officers with dogs, watching and observing, marched us out to a fenced-in area, a huge circle with a twenty-five-foot-high fence with razor wire and cameras. We could walk round for our hour or sit.

This was the only time to hustle. It was the only time to get tobacco, buy drugs, or settle scores. Everyone seemed to belong to a gang or clique. There seemed to be safety in numbers. Scousers would hang with Scousers; Mancunians and Yorkies stuck together. If someone from Bradford started a gang fight on the yard against another region, we were expected to fight, and sometimes they pitted region against region. That's how people survived.

At the end of exercise, we would begin to make our way inside. I was told this was the moment to settle a score, with huge crowds trying to get through the double doors. If someone was a grass, a rapist or a granny mugger, this was the time. Just as my cellmate was explaining this to me, bang! Someone in front of us had just been hit round the face with a small table leg that had been pulled off his table in his cell and concealed for this moment.

Bang again! The riot bells rang, and the crowds were pushing forward to see, trying to hold the officers back to give them more time to fight. Apparently, he was a grass. Inmates began to spit on him and stamp on his face before officers with dogs rescued him. Everyone was rushed back to their cells as quickly as possible, and the atmosphere changed. Adrenalin started pumping. I could sense everyone was looking for an opportunity to release their own pent-up anger.

Finally, we were all banged up again in our cells. Bullies sniffed out fear in those who looked as though they had a chink in their armour and had no backup. They'd be all over them, taking their toiletries and tobacco and beating them up. In desperation, some would be put on a protection wing with others for their own safety.

One evening a week we had the chance to get out of our cells and be taken to the church chapel to watch a film on the big screen. At this point in the eighties, the only thing we were allowed in prison was a small radio that ran on batteries, so this was the big night out. The movie was usually a thriller, and, like being at a football match, all the boys would be shouting and screaming every time there was a kiss or a short skirt. It was also a good time for anyone selling drugs to quietly wheel and deal.

Once, in the row in front of me to the right, was a tall guy with a huge beard. The lads sitting behind him were teasing him but were met with no response. Out of nowhere came a lighter, and from behind, the man's huge beard was set on fire. Immediately a fight broke out, the riot bell rang, and the place was swarming with officers running in from all directions. Everyone was kicking off. We were all spilt up into smaller groups and hurried back to our cells. I can't ever remember watching a film to the end.

Chapter 12

Life at Armley

Evenings in Armley prison were always interesting. Lying on ours beds, listening to conversations as people stood on their pipes to talk to their mates out the windows. Some nights we would hear someone screaming and smashing up their cell with anger and frustration at being trapped for so long in one place. Everyone would run to the windows to encourage the shouting to go on: "Mate, smash it up!" It was like being at a football match. People began to push their sheets through the bars in the cell to drop on the ground outside and light newspapers and drop them out to create a fire to try to burn the place down.

It only took a few minutes to go from calm to chaos. The place was electric with pent-up anger. People would rattle their cups in their bars and make gorilla-like chants. When the officers or fire brigade would come to put the fire out, inmates would spit out the windows at the officers and the firemen. Once the fire was out and the guy who smashed his cell was busted and taken to solitary confinement, everything quieted down and things began to tick as normal…well, HMP Armley-style normal.

Caged in a cell with a stranger for twenty-three hours a day meant we had to try and get on together because we were both in the same situation. If we had a disagreement for some reason and ended up in a fight, there was no one to help us or break it up. We had to sort out the issue and whoever was left standing wins. Sometimes that was the end of it, but not always.

Looking back and writing this today made me realize just how brutal prison can be. It's really survival off the fittest because if you can't fight, you're in big trouble. Time in jail always seems to go by so slowly. You live from one meal to the next as time doesn't really matter. You're not going anywhere anytime soon.

Conversations with new cellmates were always interesting, listening to them brag about past crimes and boast about the next big job on the horizon. Some people are just full of bull, and no matter what you say, they have always done better than you. If you've been to Tenerife, they have been to Eleven-a-reef. But there was nothing much more to do than talk, though our conversations were never fruitful.

Laying on my bed for hours a day gave me plenty of time to think. I recognised my life was trapped in a never-ending cycle of addiction, crime, and prison. I found going to prison was like being sentenced to criminal college, connecting with people from different places up and down the country, all swapping ideas and ways of getting in and out of places, disarming alarm systems, breaking into cars, blowing up factories, forging money…the list is endless.

I was still a first timer to the prison system. I didn't

know the score or how things worked. My cellmate, on the other hand, had been in for many years and showed me how things worked. He taught me how to make myself some lethal weapons in case I needed them.

I had already seen the first one on the exercise yard and caused some devastating damage. The second one was the trusty table leg, broken off a cell table and guaranteed maximum damage. The third way was old school but effective: putting old batteries into a sock, using pieces of metal carefully sharpened into a sharp blade, or using a razor blade.

Every prisoner was issued a cheap plastic razor to shave with, and they were allowed to keep it in their cell. Prisoners would smash it up and take out the razor blade. Then they'd melt the plastic toothbrush with matches at one end and two blades with a distance of a match between them so that when they sliced with it, it made two cuts, but only one was able to be stitched.

The final weapon was boiling hot water with sugar mixed in it to scar the face permanently. It was gruesome and not very nice to watch. It all seemed pretty savage.

These are still the weapons of choice in the prison system today, and most use them to survive. I write this to you not to boast, but so you will pray for the men who are living this right now because God loves each and every one of them with an everlasting love.

Every week we would be taken from the prison, handcuffed, put in a meat van, and driven to the local courts in our hometown. This usually meant a whole day going before the judges only to be refused bail and sent back to HMP Armley. Going to court was a long, boring day and it means a new cell and new cellmate to live with before a long wait for court again. I never knew what or where my new cell would be or who was in it, and I was stuck with that person whether we clicked or not.

Chapter 13

Judgement Day!

Finally, after many months on remand, the big day came for us: the day of judgement sentencing. All of us bundled into one huge cell with floor-to-ceiling bars. Joints were rolled as someone kept a watch and passed it around quietly. Armed robbers, murderers, burglars, car thieves, those who committed grievous bodily harm, shoplifters…all kinds of people waiting to be sentenced were crammed together in one cell.

Every hour a name would be called, and the prisoner would be handcuffed to two officers side by side, and up they went to the judges. Some came down smiling, some grown men crying, others shouting. Finally, it was our turn. Our crimes along with our previous convictions were read out loud. The brothers were sentenced one by one and sent down.

Then I stood alone in the dock. I looked defiant, ready to give the judge a mouthful of abuse. To my surprise I was given community service because I had no previous sentences. *Wow! A chance at freedom,* I thought. This time

I kept my mouth absolutely shut. I came down smiling and was released. Boy it was good. I was elated that I was free and did the only thing I knew: I immediately hooked up with the old crowd to go back to a life of drugs and crime. I hadn't lived any other way. I felt lost, so I used drugs to hide it.

While in prison, I found out I had become a father for the first time. I couldn't wait to get out, but unfortunately the relationship between me and Fiona's mum didn't work out. I was gutted but understood I was completely off the rails. I was young and out of control with no desire to change. All I wanted was to get high.

When I was finally released from prison, I moved in across the road to stay close by at a friend's house and began to make up for lost time. I was keen to put into practice all the things I had been told and shown in prison. I felt more confident than ever. The house I was staying in was only three doors down from my home where my family still lived. Other than my brothers speaking to me, there was no other real communication.

When the night came, I went out in search of a job to do. Climbing high commercial buildings and looking for the alarm system to dismantle, I would often lay quietly high in the darkness and watch the police and other traffic pass by. I would always carry a weapon in the event of any unforeseen surprises. If I triggered a hidden alarm, I would get out as fast as I could before the helicopter and the dogs arrived on the scene. If they did arrive, I would walk through streams to get rid of my scent and walk alone on the derelict train lines through the dead of night to the next town or village and try again.

I felt I had no purpose in life and didn't really care if I lived or died. I committed crimes to get high; there was no room for anything else. Life without crime and drugs seemed pointless to me.

Chapter 14

Beginnings of Addiction

One day, I struck up an interesting friendship with a guy while smoking weed. He was dealing amphetamines. He was always very paranoid, always taking his car apart looking for bugs he believed the drug squad had put in his car to hear him talking about his deals. His arms were full of holes and sores from all the hits, and his nose was in bad shape.

I had never done speed before. He got out the needle and spoon and began wrapping his belt around my arm, trying to find a good vein to shoot up. He hit it and I felt like a rocket had taken off inside me. I was rushing round awake for almost two days.

A few weeks later, he offered me a few ounces to deal for him. I was young and wanted to be the big man with all the gear, so I said "yes," thinking I was some gangster, but really, I was a messed-up teen who didn't have a clue. I took the powder and hid it behind a bath panel in the house where I was staying.

A few days later, around 4 a.m., the front door of the house was smashed off and the drug squad arresting me and searched the house. The dogs found the drugs, so it was game over. There was no doubt in my mind what would happen, and the next day I was yet again remanded into custody to that all-familiar place, the black castle on the hill HMP Armley. It lived up to its reputation as a stinking filthy hellhole.

It felt strange to be going back so soon, but part of me accepted that being locked up from time to time was just part of the life I had chosen. I was numb to it and had no intention of changing. This time I knew the score and the routine.

The next morning on exercise, I met up with old faces. Seems they too had a bad run and came back too early. Days turned to months. If I applied, once a week I could use the library. I seemed to be drawn to the weird books on the paranormal and unexplained mysteries. I had a hunger for anything dark and dangerous and a slight obsession with the devil and the darker side of life.

My mind was certainly not normal. The things that went through it were always intent on evil. My mind was so messed up I didn't feel safe in my own skin or even with my own thoughts.

Once a week we were allowed a shower. We were taken in single file to the shower blocks. This was a dodgy time and we needed to be on full alert, as rapes, fights, and drug deals had been reported there.

After about eight months, my crown court date finally came. This time my barrister told me straight out to expect three to four years; anything less would be a miracle because of my previous crimes. Hanging in the court holding cells with everyone brought hope. The people coming down with their sentences were all smiling because they all got less time than they expected. Apparently, the judge was in a good mood.

Finally, my time came. I was cuffed on either side to an officer and taken up. Rather than cussing, I tried to look as sorry as possible while my crimes were read out. Burglary, car theft, and drug possession didn't sound good. Eventually after a long lecture from the judge, I was sentenced to two and a half years in a young offender's institution. Happy, I was taken down to the cells. It had been a good day. I had received a much lighter sentence than I had expected.

After several more hours of waiting, we were all bundled in a van and enroute to the hellhole on the hill, HMP Armley. After a long day of waiting around in the prison reception area, a cold tea was presented. Then we had a cold shower and a quick strip search naked, squat and cough. I received my stinky bed blankets and was taken to my new cell to meet my new cellmate. It was good to be home.

My cellmate wasn't a weirdo, and after a quick exchange of the usual questions, he told me he had some weed for later. Bonus! Just what I needed after the final check at 9 p.m. While the keys were jangling in the distance, joints were rolled. We made bucket bongs and began to smoke them. The room was full of smoke, and we were totally stoned.

When the weed and the matches had run out, we tore the bed sheets into thin strips and tied them together to make a line to drop down to the cell beneath to get some matches. While we were at the window, shouting, the cell door suddenly burst open, and a load of officers piled in and overwhelmed us. We were busted.

It was the A Team, the night staff. We called one "sniffer" because he could sniff out drugs anywhere. Quickly we were dragged out of the cell, which was totally trashed. "You're wasting your time; it's all gone. Better luck next time," I said. We were strip searched and standing up straight with our arms behind our backs. We were told to stick our chins out, and each of us received one huge slap in the face. This was normal in the eighties; we just had to suck it up and take it on the chin.

Chapter 15
Smuggling Drugs into Armley

The next morning the prison was awakened to the same sound as every other morning: slop out! What a great way to wake up, half asleep with a bucket full of urine, waiting for my turn to swish it out and clean it. We were on the middle floor and could see the people and officers below slopping out.

Suddenly an officer shouted, "You, yes, you, tuck in your shirt, now!" Seems the lad was having none of it and the officer didn't see what was coming. The lad simply threw the contents of his bucket over the officer. The riot bell was blown, and officers everywhere began running up the stairs to grab the lad. Everyone was screaming, laughing, and shouting. Quickly he was slammed to the floor. We were banged up behind our doors. Before a riot kicked off, the lad was taking a beating and dragged to the block solitary confinement. After a few hours normal routine resumed like clockwork.

Later that morning, I was taken to stand before an allocation panel. Being newly sentenced, I was to be shipped out to HMP Ever Thorpe in ten days' time to serve out my sentence as HMP Armley was only a remands prison. I didn't receive visits from any of my family or get any mail, so my cell mate and I hatched a plan to smuggle in some drugs before I left HMP Armley. His girlfriend would come to see him, and her friend would come to see me and bring the drugs in. I would receive half the package deal to take with me to my new prison.

When the day came, we were laying on our prison bunkbeds, waiting for the visits to start at 1:30. At that time, the cell door was opened, and both our names were called. "Visits, boys. Wait downstairs." This was it. Walking over to the visits block, I felt determined and tried to look confident. I felt a mixture of excitement and nerves as I was about to meet a total stranger who was about to pass me a package of heroin and crack cocaine.

Sitting at my visiting table felt strange. All the men were looking in the direction of the door the visitors came through, waiting for their loved ones with expressions of joy on their faces. When their visitors came in, they walked to the table and hugged their relatives and loved ones.

I had one chance to make it look like I was in love with this stranger bringing me drugs. I had only seen a photograph of her. Finally, I spotted her. We could have won an Oscar as we smiled, hugged, and kissed one another.

The visiting room was packed. On the table next to me with his visitor was my cellmate. We were trying to ignore one another as the officers were patrolling up and down the aisles. At the end of the room, on either side, were officers sitting on their chairs on top of the tables to catch people smuggling.

After a polite chat, I asked the girl how big the package was. She opened her mouth and showed it to me. It looked quite large. There are only three options at the end of the visit:

1. She could kiss me and transfer the package into my mouth so I could swallow it and wait three days for it to come out of my behind.

2. I could plug it, which meant that after she passed it to me when the coast was clear, I could quickly push it into my backside to have instant access to it later.

3. I could just stuff it in my underwear and hope the officers didn't find it.

I chose the best and safest way: to plug it. Just as the visits were about to finish, we made the pass, safely and successfully.

After the visits, random searches were made. I was pulled aside and put in the "to be searched" queue, which led to a wooden platform around the corner. I watched as others were being searched. Some got a quick rub down, but others had to pull down their trousers and squat. The officers knew the score. They know people plug their gear, and if it's not plugged correctly, a squat would force it.

I was almost there. Suddenly the officers jumped on a lad and asked him to open his mouth. He refused as it was full of drugs. They pinned him to the ground, holding his throat so he couldn't swallow. He spat the drugs out and was taken to the block.

I was next. *Here goes nothing,* I thought. I stood on the wooden platform and was told to open my mouth. I got rubbed down. I was also told to unzip my pants and squat. When I did, nothing happened. I had slipped through the net and was escorted to my cell. We had done it. We laid low and quietly enjoyed the stash later that night, 50/50.

Chapter 16

Sent to Ever Thorpe

A few days later the morning came to be transferred to another prison to serve out my sentence. After a bowl of cold, sloppy prison porridge, I found myself being chained in the back of a van with others heading to the same place. We were driving for hours, and I realised I had not had any visits from family and friends. Now there would be no chance of any at all. I would have to wheel and deal and hustle to make things happen if I were to survive. Thankfully I was arriving with a small stash to start a little business in my new home.

Finally, after three and a half hours, we arrived deep in some forest in the middle of nowhere. HMP Ever Thorpe looked like every other prison from the outside: high fences covered in razor wire, security cameras, and officers patrolling with their dogs. We were soon processed, taken to a room, given a run down on the rules, and warned about the consequences of breaking them.

I was excited to be in a working prison. No more slop out, as all cells had a toilette, and no more twenty-three-hour-a-day bang ups. Here I would get a prison job or go on education, which means working from morning until evening. It also means the gym would be unlocked as would the TV room, and there were even pool tables where we could go at the end of the day. It was called "association time."

After we read the rules, we were led to our cells, bedroll in one hand and pillowcase stuffed with all our personal items in the other. Entering the landing, lads were everywhere buzzing about, weighing us up, trying to intimidate. I signalled to them I was ready, so if they had a problem to sort out, they could bring it there and then. Any sign of weakness at this moment meant being singled out and bullied.

After a couple of hours our cell door opened. We were given a scrubbing brush and a block of green wax in a bucket and taken to what is called the M1. The M1 is a huge corridor about the length of two football pitches; it was a huge narrow corridor that connected all the wings.

As new boys we had to get on our hands and knees side by side and scrub the floor with the wax and work our way down, with everyone buzzing about and walking over it, accompanied by officers. We had two choices: to keep our heads down and keep scrubbing or kick off. I chose to keep scrubbing. A few hours later we were told to go to our cells until association time from 6-8 p.m.

At 8 p.m. my cell door opened along with everyone else's. Because we were new, everyone was staring at us, as we were "fresh meat." Thankfully I recognised some old cellmates from HMP Armley. We chatted like old mates and were given the real rundown on how things work. It was just like every other jail. If we had the collateral, we could get what we wanted. Tobacco, phone cards, and food were the currency.

The night was passing nicely. There were a few options on association: chat with someone or play pool or table tennis. I joined the queue to wait patiently for a game of pool. Near the end of association time, the gate at the end of the landing opened, and about ten lads came in with an officer to use the gym. I didn't take too much notice.

Then, to my surprise, one of the lads walked straight to the pool table to the guy playing his shot, took the pool cue out of his hand, and said to him, "Beat it; I am on now." I couldn't believe it. It was a lad I knew from HMP Armley prison. We had nearly had a fight before as he would bully first timers and take their belongings. We were pulled apart once. The issue was unresolved. He had disappeared and been shipped out.

I walked over to the table, grabbed the pool cue, and told him I was on next. He tried to grab the cue from me. The place seemed to go silent. Everyone was watching. Shocked, a couple of officers quickly came and put me back in my cell to cool off. Fuming, I shouted, "I will bite your ear off in the morning!" and I meant it.

About thirty minutes later association finished, and everyone was back in their cells. The final count was done, and the officers left the wing. At that moment the place seemed to come alive with everyone shouting out of their windows. Then someone in the cell underneath me began banging on the ceiling and shouting out the window. It was brownie the Rasta, the lad I had the scuffle with at the pool table.

"Rowan, I am going to bust your face in tomorrow!" he mouthed off.

"I will see you in the morning then!" I replied.

For the next hour I was listening to him running his mouth, telling anyone who would listen just what he was going to do to me. Seemed I had made it through my first day, but the second would be much more interesting. I didn't sleep much that night as I was full of rage. I often scared myself with the violent thoughts that rushed through my mind.

I was up at sunrise, ready to fight and to pack up all my possessions in the world, which were toiletries and a few letters, ready for solitary confinement.

Chapter 17

28 Days of Solitary

Eventually, my cell door was opened for breakfast. I was on the second floor, looking down. There was brownie still giving it loads and telling me to come. He was dressed from head to toe in a white kitchen uniform, which means he has a job serving food. Sure enough, he was serving the breakfast.

I picked up my metal tray from the pile, looking for one with a sharp edge. Holding the tray, I refused the cornflakes and the milk. The only thing I wanted was blood. He was next in line. I swung the tray at his face, looking to cause serious damage. I jumped up on the servery, sending crockery and breakfast flying in all directions, and launched myself over the counter toward him, aiming a punch at his head and trying to get my teeth in his face. I could see he was shocked.

Immediately the riot bells and whistles went off. Officers came from everywhere and jumped on me. Adrenalin pumping, I could hear people shouting and being banged up as I was smothered in officers. Two had my arms behind my back, and two more were forcing my shoulders and head to the floor. They dragged me all the way down the M1, threw me into a very dark cell, pinned me to the floor, and punched me.

I was still struggling whilst being held down. They cut my clothes off me with a large pair of scissors, and soon I was left naked. They threw me what looked like an old large potato sack with corners cut off and a hole in the middle for my head. I put it on. The door slammed. I was alone, bruised, and battered in a dark room.

Sitting in the dim, silent darkness, I had no sense of time, so I didn't know if it was day or night. I began to work out the time by meals. At night I was given a very thin mattress that was taken away in the morning and replaced with a table and chair made of pressed cardboard. There was nothing else, only complete silence.

Looking back at these things I have done has made me realise how angry, broken, and lost I really was.

The next morning the cell door opened, and two officers escorted me into a mini court room to face the prison governor. Opposite the desk sat the prison governor with an officer on either side of him. I had to stand on a line with my hands behind my back with an officer on either side of me. An officer on duty the morning of the fight gave his account of the event, and I pleaded guilty. Twenty-eight days were added to my sentence, plus I had to serve twenty-eight days in solitary confinement. I also lost two weeks' pay, which is about four pounds. Thirty a week doesn't sound like much, but inside it is.

The twenty-eight days seemed like a lifetime of pure boredom. Alone in that cell, I created a routine of daily exercise for myself and saved processed peas from my meals to dry out and play games like marbles, which sounds absolutely crazy, but it kept me sane.

Eventually the twenty-eight days of solitary passed, and I was taken back to the same wing I had left and back to my old cell. It seemed I had won some respect. I saw brownie, who I had the fight with. He avoided me, which was cool with me, as our score seemed to have been settled.

Now back on the wing, I was finally allowed my gym induction, so I could focus on fitness to pass the time. Ever Thorpe had an assault course in the middle of the M1, which was a real killer. The gym instructors were ruthless. They sat us down, gave us a pep talk, and demonstrated what we needed to do on each piece of equipment.

Then we were lined up, and when the whistle blew, we were off around the obstacle course, stopping at each station to do press ups, sit ups, squats…you name it. We had to keep moving, no stopping allowed. Over benches, under benches, up the ropes, down the ropes, the pace was quick.

In the middle of the room was a huge metal bucket to throw up in, and many did, including myself. It was brutal, but we soon got fit.

Chapter 18

Full-Scale Riot

Prison routine gets boring after a while. We had heard on the radio that other young-offender prisons had rioted. So, the whole prison began planning a full-scale riot to wreck the place, smash up the wing, and attack the officers. There were four wings to the prison, two at the bottom of the M1 and two at the top, shaped like the letter I, with about one hundred and fifty lads on each wing. A plan and a signal were hatched.

The signal to kick off would happen during association time after work when all the prisoners would be out. The signal to go for it would be when someone set off the fire alarms.

All day we could feel the anger, hate, and anticipation building. Everyone was whispering about it and bragging about which officer they were going to beat up and take hostage. Weapons were made ready for the evening: holes were cut out of pillowcases and turned into balaclavas and were hidden away and ready.

When work finished that day, we were all banged up in our cells for role check. We behaved ourselves as usual for teas, and everything carried on as normal until we were unlocked for association time. People were playing pool and chatting but intently waiting for the signal. Some lads were hanging about close to the officers, leaning against a wall and chatting, ready to attack and take the keys to try to escape when the bell went.

Other lads had planned to get the keys to make it to the hospital wing to unlock the main drug cabinet and get high. Still others were just intent on going crazy and smashing the place up.

An hour passed. Everyone was getting impatient. Is it going to kick off or what? I made the mistake of checking out the TV room at the end of the landing. It was full of about twenty-five lads watching TV with an officer standing at the back. Finally, the bell rang, and all hell let loose. The officer slammed the TV room door and locked us in. We were trapped. They knew what was going to happen out on the landing and were waiting for it.

Everyone was going crazy. Pool balls were being thrown at officers. Everything was being smashed. Everyone was waging their own private battle. Inside the TV room chairs were being thrown against the wall and against the lights on the ceiling. Glass was flying everywhere. I had lost it and was screaming, "Come on!" I started headbutting the windows in a complete rage.

With the lights smashed, we were in total darkness but could just about make out each other's faces. Everyone seemed to be getting rid of pent-up frustrations. Suddenly through the TV room windowless door through the bars, we could see the riot squad running toward us in full riot gear. They had been waiting, dressed all in black with helmets, truncheons, and shields. They were in some weird formation like an arrowhead side by side. Those at the front were banging their truncheons against their riot shields. They had a reputation for not messing about.

Everyone started throwing the chairs toward the door. Others quickly began to make a barricade with the chairs until they were all piled high. There was only one way in and one way out: this door. Lighters were flickering to see better. I felt my face; it was cold and wet. I was covered in blood. The windows had left a wide gash on my forehead. I took off my t-shirt and tied it around my head to stop the bleeding.

After a long standoff and few hours had passed, through a broken window we demanded to see the prison governor. Eventually he came, and we made request of a news film crew and better food, but he refused all our requests. We were trapped. We were told to move the chairs and promised there would be no beating from the riot squad. We held out a little longer, but eventually we agreed and surrendered.

When all the chairs had been removed, they called for the injured to come out first with our hands above our heads, one at a time. Once I made it out, I was escorted into a side office and laid on a desk with jell-like congealed blood all over me. My cut was cleaned, and I was given seven stitches and locked back in my cell for the next week or so. We were banged up more than usual while the clean-up had finished, and new windows and lights were put back in.

Everything slowly began returning to the boring routine of prison life. My first year went very slowly, but then the months flew by quickly and my time for release was near. I had made many contacts and had learned many things. I was keen to put them all into action. It was as though I had gone to the college for criminals to learn new skills on how to commit more crimes.

Chapter 19

Life of Crime and Addiction

Finally, the day of my release came. I was given a discharge grant because I was now twenty years old. I had applied for a flat near where I used to live in Brooklyn in Cleckheaton, and I was given my first home. On the morning of my release, we were taken to the train station and left there. I caught the train with another lad who had just been released. We bought alcohol and began to celebrate.

Brooklyn was well known for drugs: cannabis, speed, pills, acid, ecstasy...anything I wanted. There were at least eight high blocks of flats full of people getting high on every block. I headed straight there, forgetting to pick up the keys to my own flat. All I wanted to do was to get stoned. First port of call was Kenny's flat. Kenny was an old hippie in his 60s, and his flat was always full of aging hippies with big beards, long hair, and flowery waistcoats.

As usual the room was filled with a cloud of smoke. Bongs and pipes were being passed round, pills were being popped, and empty beer cans were all over the place. The guitar would be passed round, and most would play it and sing. It was filthy, but it felt good to finally be free. I had no plans for the future other than to live in the moment. Kenny was an eccentric. He had a dog called Monday, so named because he found it on a Monday, and he used to get all his food from the local skips. He would bring anything weird or trippy home and glue it to the ceiling or to the walls.

The next day I picked up the keys for my flat. It felt good to have my own place. I tried to make it a home, but a few days into my freedom I bumped into an old mate called Phil, and we were to become inseparable partners in crime. He was an absolute psychopath, and the first time I met him, he had part of someone's ear on his mantle piece. He had bitten it off an enemy in a fight he'd had recently. He had stabbed countless people and had quite a reputation. We got high and we were close friends for many years.

Once we had some money, the flat became utter chaos, far from the home I had envisioned. The parties started, and people from other blocks would come over to join us. Some were snorting lines of speed on a small mirror. Others were cooking drugs on spoons in the kitchen and shooting up on the sofa and in the chairs. Sometimes I didn't leave the flat for days.

All my life I had felt driven by an unseen force that wanted to destroy my life, and I was happy to enjoy the ride and let it all happen. I had no idea I was born with a purpose and that I had a destiny. I knew only the darkness.

At night, gangs from the local clubs would come to the flat singing and shouting after the night clubs had closed. We would also climb on top the roof and pass up stereos while people continued the party. We were fifteen floors up, so if anyone had slipped, they would have had no chance of survival certain death. The police often came but could do nothing.

During one party, my brother, Danny, had too much to drink. We hung him off the top by his hand and swung him out and in, building momentum, so he would hopefully swing into the bathroom window below.

I was offered the opportunity to begin dealing again, and of course I said, "yes." Phil and I took the stuff from flat to flat, selling it and using it at the same time, leaving behind us a trail of flats crowded with people getting high. We had to carry weapons so that if other dealers tried to set up shop on our patch, we would be straight on it. Turf wars were common. If you lost your turf, you lost your income.

Magic mushroom season was soon upon us. Groups of us would go to the fields and spend hours hunting for magic mushrooms. Some wild mushrooms contain psilocybin, which gives a powerful hallucinogenic effect similar to LSD. I would usually go with Kenny, the hippie, because he was more experienced. Even as we were picking them, we would start to feel high as the psilocybin made its way in through the pores of our skin.

We would go home happy after a carrier bag was full, knowing what the night had in store. At the flat we would make tea out of the mushrooms. Then we would hold tight for the next five hours as the hallucinations kicked in slowly, soon to land on another planet of swirling, moving sea carpets, talking wallpaper, and furniture turning into strange looking animals. They totally blew our heads clean off. Those who had a bad trip would start seeing devils and demons and all kinds of bad stuff.

Most nights I would go burgling if I was able to walk or focus. I often went alone, but if I was planning to hit a big factory with many offices, an extra pair of hands were needed. I learnt a lot about dismantling alarms systems when I was in prison. I would usually dismantle the alarm from the roof, then retreat and watch for a while. If no police came, we knew we were safe and could take our time.

We would move together from room to room, dismantling and unplugging equipment and moving it to the door, ready for pickup. Finally, we would transfer the goods to a safe place and call our buyer, who would meet us at 5 a.m. Then we would strike a cash deal, load it up, and go home to bed, knowing the stuff was gone and we were no longer connected to the job.

I was a terrible thief. I didn't seem to care about my life. Drugs seemed to hide the pain and fill the emptiness I felt inside for a short time. I would steal anything that wasn't screwed down. If I wanted something, I would go out and get it. If I was passing a shop and saw a bike outside, I would jump on it and ride it. I was disrespectful and arrogant.

During the day, people would be window shopping for nice things and living normal lives. My normal day was to get high, as well as dodge the police and my enemies, and then find weaknesses in properties, such as restaurants, snooker halls, and even nightclubs so I could hit them at nightfall.

Sometimes if we missed a floor sensor and the alarms screamed out, we ran through fields, back alleys, and streams to escape the helicopters, dogs, and police cars. Once we had a clear distance from the scene and calmed down, we would walk silently along the railway lines to the next town to try again, driven by the need to get high again.

Day or night, if seen by the police, I would be stopped and searched for weapons, drugs, or outstanding warrants. I began to leave equipment hidden all over town: screwdrivers in peoples garden hedges, crowbars in graveyards, other tools on the roofs of various shops and commercial buildings, as well as knives and weapons to protect myself.

Quite often the drug squad would kick the door off and ransack my flat, looking for drugs or the proceeds of crime. Friends in other high-rise flats would often tip me off that the cops were on their way to mine. Immediately I would go underground at night under darkness and move from house to house. I had many close shaves with the police.

Writing this now, I can see why I was a menace to society and needed serious help. But anytime the police caught up with me, I made things as difficult as possible.

While I was being fingerprinted and photographed, and the hard evidence, along with the accompanying charges, were stacked against me, I would always remain silent in court, but only until I heard the verdict. If I got sent back to prison, I would often shout at the judges, but my solicitor would always put up a good fight for me. I had come to know the courts very well and knew the maximum they could give.

On this occasion I somehow got a probation order for two years and was ordered to pay compensation. I knew at that moment I would not attend or pay before leaving the court room. Angry that I walked, the police soon let me know that they would be watching me and that they would eventually put me down for many years. I gave them a nice smile, a few choice words of my own, and the middle finger and carried on as usual.

My buddy and I decided to have a drink in the area where I was most wanted. Soon a fight broke out in the toilettes and one guy got hurt badly. The next evening a car and a van of lads armed with machetes and baseball bats were banging on the doors of all the local crack houses, looking to kill us. We were tooled up with bats and blades and ready, but we were well outnumbered and would have gotten seriously hurt if they had caught up with us.

This was the chaos and the madness I was living in, but in those crazy days I didn't care if I lived or died. In fact, death would be a relief from the crazy life I was living.

After a few days and things calmed down, I felt the need to get a normal job and straighten myself out. Both would be miracles.

Chapter 20

Giving a Go at Work

Finally, the opportunity did come for me to work, and I gave a good go, but I was so dependent on the drugs that I was weak, I looked like a zombie, and I had no energy whatsoever. It all went pear shaped from day one and I was fired.

I didn't get another job for quite some time until an old friend, Tim, came on the scene.

Tim was an addict but also a builder by trade. He told me he had managed to secure a contract for work on a house and asked if my friends and I needed work. We said "yes" and arranged to meet the next morning and go to the site together. The house was a mess. The walls needed rebuilding and plastering, a chimney needed to be knocked down, electrics needed to be put in, and so on.

Once Tim had explained the work needed, we decided the plan of action was to snort a line of coke and roll a joint to get started. Later the owner of the house, who owned a shop, came with tea bags, but after some time, we convinced him that builders needed beer, and he brought a whole crate to the site.

That evening, at a smoking session, we hired two friends to start work with us the next day, one to do the electrics and the other to roll joints, get our lines on the mirror ready for snorting, and make cups of tea when needed. It soon became apparent that our long-haired hippy electrician knew absolutely nothing about electrics, as we caught him stuffing unconnected wires into the sockets and hiding it all by screwing on a power socket. But we left him to it. I guess we all knew it wasn't going to work out.

That afternoon we managed to bag a few more grand for materials, caught a taxi to the strip clubs, got stoned, and went home. People were angry and looking for us, but we were so out of it that we just decided to stay tooled up, take it as it comes, and deal with the situation when it arises.

The police were looking to arrest me yet again. I had been charged with assault and resisting arrest, and I was bailed, but failed to appear at court. I was also on my final warning for not turning up for probation appointments. I had to tread carefully as I knew my feet wouldn't touch the ground if the police found me. I would be remanded into custody at HMP.

My neighbours were constantly complaining, and the council eventually moved me to another block across the road. Although it was the smallest block in Brooklyn, it was also the worst, as all dealers lived in it. On the first floor were cannabis dealers, and opposite his front door, another lad dealt acid and speed. On the floor above me lived an ecstasy dealer.

At night the block never seemed to sleep. There was a constant flow of people coming and going. My brother, Danny, had also moved into the first floor of the block.

My new flat resembled what was going on inside my head. It had black carpets. There were broken buddhas and burnt-out joss sticks everywhere. After cleaning up the place and hanging trippy psychedelic posters everywhere, I was given a Doberman pincher. They had quite a reputation, so I accepted, hoping I could train it to bite any unwanted drug squads or policemen with arrest warrants. In a chair in the corner of the room I also installed a human skeleton, which I'd stolen from some college laboratory. It was held together by a metal clip. It had a rubber snake going through its eyes, a fake joint in its mouth, one hand made of a radio and knife blade for an aerial, and the other bony hand was wrapped round an acoustic guitar.

My mind wasn't ok. There was no mention of mental health in the eighties and nineties. I was warped, confused, and out of control with no zeal for life and no vision. I just couldn't see a future. I had sadly come to terms that one day I would spend the rest of my life in prison, die of an overdose, or be murdered. It just didn't seem possible to live a normal life without a miracle. I didn't know it, but that is exactly what was going to happen.

I started to go to raves, which were starting to spring up in and around Leeds. It was new to everyone and full on. The raves were always jam packed with about 150 people with glowsticks and smiley t-shirts, dancing around and going crazy in their own little worlds. Music was always pumping, and there were always plenty of people selling acid, coke, and ecstasy around the clubs. I bought some and was soon hallucinating. I felt as though I had been wired up to some invisible socket.

Strobe lights flashing and smoke machines kicking out fog seemed very weird, but after four or five hours, everyone spilled onto the streets, pupils like dustbin lids and high as kites. People just didn't know what to do, where to go, or how to speak much that made any sense.

Eventually we piled into a taxi and were on our way home. Nothing seemed real. The taxi window wobbled like cellophane. The roads seemed to be painted luminous. I couldn't look at the driver because his face was too big for his body. Once we were home, pipes were passed round until the big comedown finally hit us.

The next day I felt as though I had been run over by a combine harvester. I was feeling low and depressed, but I was hooked on the rave scene for quite some time until it started taking its toll on my body. I was so skinny and didn't look well. On a few occasions, I tried to take an overdose of strong tablets to die, but I always woke up. I thought my body had built up such a high immunity to drugs that I couldn't overdose. But God had a great plan for my life, and he wasn't going to let me destroy it.

Chapter 21

Arrested, Charged… and Released!

Things were about to change. Having emptied yet another warehouse, we stashed the gear in a friend's flat. Since we were having trouble getting a buyer for all the TVs, computers, faxes, printers, and camcorders filling up the flat, the following morning we went out in search of a buyer.

We left our address with a potential buyer, and later that day a man in everyday overalls turned up at the flat and asked us if he could look at the gear. High and keen to sell, we let him in. After viewing the gear for a moment, he made a call to someone and said the gear was good to go. It was a setup. Immediately police cars, both marked and plain, as well as police vans all screeched up the street and surrounded the house. We were caught red handed by the regional crime squad, cuffed, and taken to the station, spiting and shouting. I knew the police would ask for a three-day lie-down, which means we were required to stay at the police station for three days of questioning about the job we were arrested for and many others.

I had been through the routine many times before, and as usual I refused to answer any questions by replying "no" to everything. If I could have reached the microphone attached to the wall, I would have bitten it off, and if could have reached the tape I would have turned it off.

The police hated me, and I hated them. They would charge me whether I was guilty or not. They would wake me all through the night for random interviews, trying to break me, but I gave the nothing-apart-from-verbal-abuse and "no" reply.

The exercise yard was a small cage in which we could walk round in a circle. It didn't take long before the withdrawals from the drugs kicked in before I felt weak, sick, depressed, and empty but I was determined the world wouldn't see my real pain, so I put on a mask.

On the third day I was handcuffed to the police reception area to wait to be transported to court. Finally, I was loaded into the horsebox, which was a van divided into tiny, one-person cells made of steel, just enough room for one person to sit or stand with steel bars. There was a lot of shouting as everyone greeted one another with the usual question, "What you in for?" Although we made light of our crimes, underneath was a lot tension, anger, and questions about whether we would make it home on bail that day or go to prison.

The van stopped at the lights, and, wanting to cause destruction, we all began rocking the van inside our little steel cells, shouting and laughing as we tried to tip the vehicle over. When we arrived in court, we were taken in two at a time and put in the holding cells, some in three-men cells and others in the cage. We had to wait hours until our cases were called. By now the jailers knew our names and we knew theirs.

As the morning wore on, the police came to let me know they were there. We were given time to speak to our solicitors, which was a chance to get tobacco from them before court. I usually asked for a shot at bail. I had had the same solicitor for a long time, and he always laid it on the line for me whether I had a realistic chance of bail or not. This time he didn't hold out much hope.

Finally, after three or four hours in the cage, my name was shouted to approach and face the judge. I was handcuffed to a friend who was to go into court after me. He told me if the judge sent him to jail, he was going to slip the cuffs off and make a run for his freedom. In the past many people had tried to jump over the dock at court and run past the judges and solicitors to the door for freedom. Only a few ever made it.

In court, my solicitor put up a good fight for my application for conditional bail, which meant a curfew and residing at one an address. Plus, I had to sign my name at the police station three times a week. It was a good shout, but it was rejected. I would have never stuck to it anyway. I was remanded into custody.

For the first time in history every prison was filled to the brim, so instead of going to prison, we were remanded to stay locked up in the local police cells. For the next couple of months, I continued to go court every two weeks to try for bail, but it was always rejected. Finally, my case was committed to the crown for sentencing.

The big day came round quick, and finally I was taken to Leeds crown court for sentencing. I was in front of the judges quite quickly. The gallery was backed with media waiting for tasty stories, along with barristers, prosecutors, and onlookers.

After I stood and gave my name and my charges were read, I had to wait for my previous convictions to be read before the judge would sentence me. With my record and behaviour no doubt I should have gone to prison for a long time, but by some miracle I was spared. When my sentence was passed, to my surprise I was given only 180 hours of community service and a fine. I couldn't believe it!

I don't think anyone was sent to prison that day in the cells. Everyone was given another form of punishment. I can only guess that the prisons were full as were all the police cells up and down the country with people who were meant to be in jail. Nevertheless, I was free once again. The police were not happy and told me privately so.

Chapter 22

Party!

That night I had a huge party. I wasn't much of a drinker but decided to go for a drink with a friend in town. We were sitting and drinking when a woman shouted, "That's him!" pointing at me. We got to chatting and discovered she was a hairdresser named Jenny, who had cut my hair one time. After talking for a while, she announced that she and a couple of mates were on a night shift and had gone to the pub on their late meal break, but they had to get back to work.

She said she was cold and asked to borrow my jumper. I gave it to her, leaving me bare-chested in the pub. Laughing and taking my jumper with her, she ran down the street with her friends, through the gates to a factory yard. I gave chase. I was cold and not amused, and I wanted it back.

I opened the factory door wearing only jeans and shoes and began to walk around in search of my jumper. People working on machines stopped and stared in disbelief. Eventually I found her at her machine, retrieved my jumper, and left the building. She was fired, and an unusual friendship began.

The next day there was a knock on my door. To my amazement, it was Jenny. She invited herself in and began looking round the place. Without warning she pushed open my bedroom door, which was full of stolen goods, and walked inside. She knew I was a burglar and wanted to help sell the gear. Little did I know at that moment we would be together in a stormy love-hate relationship for years to come. We began smoking cannabis and snorting powder.

Some nights she would come out burgling with me. I would dismantle the alarm, and she would go to the second floor and unplug everything, getting it all ready to go. As usual, getting high would follow. Some nights we would make Ouija boards and try to talk to any available dead spirits. The glass would move backward and forward as we asked questions. Weird stuff happened.

After being sacked, Jenny could no longer pay her rent and moved in with me at Brooklyn. We would go out shopping, using stolen credit cards, and sell the merchandise we purchased. At this point in my life, my arms, feet, hands, and neck were full of track marks from the needles. I was a complete wreck of a person.

Money was always scarce, so we began dealing LSD. I would buy a hundred acid tabs at a time and sell them for a few quid. Each tab was three or four hours of hallucinations. It seemed everyone wanted it. It was also magic mushroom season again, so we made tea with mushrooms for anyone visiting the house, and they were left to trip the night away.

My flat was just a house for junkies and never really a home. The early hours would soon come around, and the trippers would begin to leave the flat once they saw the morning light. I would take my guitar and my dog and find a place to play alone, watching the sun coming up hoping I would never come down to face the reality of life.

The police kept their word, and early one morning I was awakened to the sound of the drug squad kicking the front door off again and charging in wearing full riot gear and carrying shields with bottles of CS gas at the ready. Thankfully they found only minute traces of drugs, bongs, and pipes. Nonetheless, they were disappointed. I would mock them for their bad timing and bad planning, but once again they vowed to come back.

Chapter 23

Heroin and Drug Dens

The next few years were the darkest of all. It was around this time I became aware of heroin coming into the area. It was new on the scene and only a few had it. I finally got hold of some and learnt how to chase the dragon for the first time. Putting this strange, weird brown powder on tin foil and burning it from underneath turned it into a running liquid, which was sucked up through an aluminium tube. The liquid ran up and down the foil when tilted.

Smoking heroin suddenly became a regular occurrence, and I began shooting it up my arms with a needle, hitting any vein possible, seeking that spaced-out feeling. Little did I know that in less than a year, everyone on the drug scene, including me, would be addicted to heroin.

I started travelling to Bradford in search of the drug. At first, I found many drugs dealers, many of whom were rip-off merchants selling anything in wraps that resembled heroin. On one visit to Bradford, I scored some crack cocaine and discovered I liked it a lot. It was very strong and deadly addictive. It was an instant high but soon left me chasing the high and wanting more.

Bradford was changing. There were more prostitutes than usual on the street corners. Chatting to them, it was obvious we were in the same boat. Nine out of ten of them needed their fix of heroin. Some were withdrawing, the pain obvious on their faces. Heroin was slowly taking over, and dealers were springing up all over the place.

Through the day, drugs would be sold from my flat. I would still also go out, looking to break into any properties available, needing to feed my ever-growing heroin and crack cocaine habit. I was a mess and would steal anything anywhere to get hold of money to buy heroin. My body was wrecked. I didn't seem to have any emotions at all for all the crimes I was committing. I could only think of getting the drugs before the sweats and the pain eventually came. I was a slave to an unseen master.

All the drugs dens I visited, were littered with bloody syringes, dirty swabs, spoons with soot all over them, spent filters, and dirty foil where people had smoked it instead of injecting it. Inexperience led to many people missing their veins and their arms swelling up like golf balls. Determination not to lose the heroin in the syringe meant trying to hit a different vein until the barrel was empty. Some would fall to the floor, shaking and sweating as though they were having a fit.

Sometimes one would steal the heroin from the one shaking on the floor and run off with it before they came around. If they didn't come around, they were carried out of the house and dumped on the street. That may sound cold and ruthless, but it's the truth and still happens today.

Jenny became pregnant. We stopped dealing acid and cannabis and started dealing heroin to support our ever-growing habits. I would wake up in the morning, sweating in pain, desperate for a fix. I had a problem and didn't know how to fix it. Other friends in Brooklyn were feeling the same. They began to sell off their TVs, stereos, cars, even their wedding rings, to raise just enough money for a fix.

There was no more respect for one another; it was survival. Grown men would cry to share a fix with someone. I tried to get help from a doctor and was registered as an addict. I was put on a high methadone script, which I had to pick up daily.

One day I was offered a large amount of heroin to start dealing in the area. Immediately I took the large sum of money and blew it on crack cocaine and partying. A few days later a gang was in the area, looking for me, armed to the teeth, kicking doors in, and threatening people who knew me to tell them where I was. A contract was out on my life. They wanted crushed bones and blood unless I had the money.

Chapter 24

Jenny and Roxanne

As Jenny was pregnant, we moved but not far. The gang soon tracked us to our new address, and two armed men were kicking the door in, threatening Jenny with hammers, and vowing to return.

When I found out, I got hold of a pump-action shotgun and, under the cover of darkness, took the back streets across town to the house where I knew the men might be. I banged on the door as a light was on. Ready, I had no intention of shooting them, just to warn them not to come back. At the least I would have blown a hole in their car parked outside to warn them, but that could all change if I were attacked.

We banged on the door again, but no answer came, so we carefully engraved their names onto a live bullet and posted through the letter box to let them know that we knew the address and that we had been there. Thankfully they never came back.

I was given the name of a new a contact in Bradford to get some gear. I will never forget the estate where we got it. It was worse than anywhere I had ever been, and I had lived in some rough places. There were empty needles on the pavement, burnt-out cars left abandoned, and wild gypsy horses just walking the streets and eating grass in people's gardens. Most of the houses had steel shutters to keep people from getting in.

There were also empty houses that had been gutted of everything: windows, doors, roof tiles, wiring…you name it. They were just empty hollow crack houses now. Even the paving slabs were all missing the paths at the side of the road as they could be sold.

Standing on the street corners were small gangs of teens taking turns to fly round the block on what was clearly a stolen motorbike. Mothers would fly past on a quad bike with kids hanging on the back to go to the shops. The mums would keep the engine running while the kids ran in to get whatever they needed. Over a period of time, we met a lot of contacts.

It was a simple friendship: we wanted the drugs, and they wanted the money. If they could rip us off, they would. If we could rip them off, we would too. Sometimes there were stabbings, so we always went armed with a weapon and took a pair of scales to weigh the heroin and a needle to shoot up to test it. By now our habits were growing steadily.

Jenny was very pregnant by this time and in the middle of the night gave birth to our daughter, Roxanne. It was the most amazing thing I had ever seen. She was beautiful. I couldn't wait for her to come home. I vowed to change and never take drugs again. I believed it with all my heart and head, but the withdrawal pains, the cramps, and the sweats became too much, and I was off to score.

Thankfully Roxanne was born with no addiction.

Just when things were looking ok, we had a huge fight at home, and I was told I would never see Roxanne again. I couldn't bear it and decided to take my own life. I felt like I couldn't go on living with no future or purpose. I took a huge overdose but survived because my body took whatever I threw at it.

The next day, weary, weak, and withdrawing from crack cocaine and heroin, I ripped the boards off a derelict building nearby. I knew well it was cold, damp, dark, and full of rubbish. This was probably the lowest point in my life. Walking around, I found a window ledge about four feet off the ground within reach and a roof beam with a metal hook sticking out from it. I contemplated my death and surrendered to it.

I wrote a note to Jenny and Roxanne, folded it, and wrote on the outside in big letters, "I AM DEAD INSIDE THE BUILDING." I placed the note on the pavement on the side of the road where I knew it would be found.

I quickly ran inside, climbed onto the ledge, made a noose from the scarf round my neck plus another I used to hide my face from the police, and tied it to the hook. In tears, I sat on the ledge for at least an hour. I knew if I jumped off that ledge, I was fully committed. I was hoping my neck would break before I suffocated. I counted down: 10, 9, 8, 7, 6, 5, 4, 3, 2, 1, and then I fully committed and jumped.

In those few moments many things ran through my mind. I was spinning around, my legs kicking wildly. I could feel I was taking my last breath as the pressure built up, and I was passing out when suddenly I felt a huge thud on the side of my face. The scarf had snapped, and I was lying on the ground, having a fit. Gasping for breath, I was pulling at the scarf around my neck to breathe again.

Instantly, as I lay on the floor, I became aware that the room was filled with what sounded like a thousand different loud voices speaking in languages I had never heard. They became increasingly louder but sounded reassuring. As I pulled the scarf off my neck and began to breathe again, the voices vanished.

I instantly felt both peace and strength. All of a sudden, my mind seemed clear, and I realised the severity of the situation. I knew something had just happened to me that was either important or some kind of weird trip from all the drugs. I never understood the experience, nor did I ever tell anyone about it or what I tried to do that day until many years later when I came to faith in Jesus in 1999.

When I gave my life to Jesus and I heard someone speak in tongues for the first time, my heart melted, and tears ran down my face as I instantly recognised it was the same language and sound that filled the room that day and brought me comfort as I tried to die. I've often wondered if I heard the prayers of intercessors, the sound of angels, or God himself. One day I will know the answer.

That day I ran from that place, quickly picking up my hat and destroying the letter. Shortly thereafter, I made my way to a friend's flat and soon had a belt around my arm, trying to find a vein to shoot up my heroin. *In just a moment everything will be ok,* I thought.

Chapter 25

The Never-ending Cycle

A few days later, Jenny and I were back together. As I was coming home, from a distance I could see the drug squad busting in the house and the place swarming with police cars and police dog vans. Immediately all kinds of things ran through my mind: *Jenny will go to prison and Roxanne will be taken into the care of local authorities.* She was arrested and I went to ground. Thankfully Jenny's mum heard of the situation and obtained custody of Roxanne. I knew it would be a long time before I would be able to see her again.

Jenny was released on bail, and a few days later the police tracked me down again and at 4 a.m. I was awakened to them smashing down my friend's door as a helicopter hovered above and armed police burst into the room. There was no bulb in the light, so it was quite dark. Police were shouting, "Don't move!" Looking down at my chest, I could see it covered with red dots from the guns. I knew it was game over. I was arrested again and charged with perverting the course of justice for threatening and intimidating witnesses along with more burglaries.

At court I was remanded into custody yet again. My life seemed to be stuck in a cycle of the same things happening over and over: drugs, crime, prison; drugs, crime, prison. All the way to jail fear gripped my whole body, not because I was returning to prison but because I was about to go through the imminent sweats, cramps, and withdrawal pains from the crack and heroin. They were every addict's nightmare.

When we arrived at the prison, there was only one thing on my mind: avoiding withdrawal at all costs. I had to get hold of some heroin fast or see the prison doctor. Most people coming into the prison would also be starting to withdraw. One by one we would see the doctor and be given a DF tablet dihydrocodeine to take the edge off. Even though it contained codeine, it did nothing for me as my habits were far too big.

After four hours of being processed—the usual cold shower, hands behind the head, squat and cough routine—I was given a warm tea and handed a stinky, dirty bedroll. Then we were taken to our cells. My last hope now would be that my cellmate, whoever that might be, may have something to help.

The usual stink of urine filled my lungs and assaulted what was left of my senses as people were slopping out.

Finally, I arrived at my cell. The door was opened and empty, and whoever was on the other bed was to be my cellmate twenty-three hours a day.

The door slammed behind me. Finally, it was opened, and my new cellmate walked in. I Introduced myself and, in desperation, instantly confessed my dilemma. He couldn't help me, so it was to be a very long, painful night ahead. I could already feel the sweat pouring down my face and from my armpits. My nose was running. One moment I felt freezing cold, the next too hot. I was in serious pain as if someone was stabbing me with a cold, sharp knife in my guts and turning it to make sure. I was constantly trying to vomit but to no avail.

I paced up and down the cell, pressing my body against the cold wall to cool down. I couldn't stay in one position for more than a few seconds. There was no peace. I felt as though I was dying. I lay on my bed, wanting the earth to swallow me, wishing the scarf had never broken. I thought about heroin constantly. Every few seconds the cramps and pain in the legs would cause me to kick out in search of relief, but there was none. Soon I was lying naked on the cell floor and then vomiting on my hands and knees, sweating, hallucinating. I wanted to scream. I wanted to die.

People were passing drugs to each other on pieces of string outside the windows, like vultures in desperation. Someone would steal the line and take what was on it, willing to accept the consequences in the morning. Hours passed. I was still awake when the sun came up, the birds began singing, and the keys began rattling again as the officers returned to work to start another day.

Chapter 26

Finding Heroin

Hope kicked in as another day started with only one thing on my mind: finding heroin. At breakfast the cell door opened, and the hustle and bustle began. Many were queuing up with buckets full of poo and urine. Others were shouting across landings, swapping newspapers, the latest porn magazines, rizlas, and tobacco. There was always someone I knew from a previous sentence who could fill me in on who had what. I could also tell who was withdrawing, the ones who looked like me: skinny, unshaven, smelly, white-faced black-eyed zombies looking frantically for a fix. Minutes later it was all over, and I was banged up in my cell again.

There was only one more chance in an hour's time during exercise, that is if it wasn't raining, to get hold of any drugs. I would need tobacco or a phone card to barter with. A tiny bag of heroin cost three phone cards, worth six pounds, or the equivalent in tobacco. Prisoners were entitled to four pounds, twenty a week. Many cellmates got together to buy a small bag of heroin that lasted just minutes and went without the rest of the week. At exercise I was able to find someone to give me a small bag on the condition that I returned twice as much. Things had changed, seemed as though it had a grip on most people. Gone were the days of weed.

It took a whole week before I had my first visit at the prison. Visits stirred up a whole range of emotions, excitement, anticipation, desperation, and fear. The cell door opened, and the guard shouted, "Rowan Visit!" The first thought that went through my head was, *Have they got me some gear?* because that was all that mattered. As I waited at the bottom of the stairs with all the lads' palms beginning to sweat, the banter was always the same: "Am I getting sorted on this visit?" Everyone kept a close eye on who was on visits in case they had something to sell when they got back to the wing.

The visit was always a tricky operation because the officers knew the score and a lot of people tried to smuggle drugs in. They also knew who was on medication and whether they had been caught before. I am given a bright yellow bib and a table number to sit at. Walking into the visiting room was always an experience. It was full of about forty lads with their visitors, plus the screams of kids. The waft of perfume for the first time in weeks was sweet to the senses. Lads, still waiting for their visitors' empty tables, shouted across to one another while the officers kept a watchful eye.

Still withdrawing and looking very ill, Jenny walked in. She had gotten bail. We hugged, and she smiled at me, showing me that in between her teeth was a parcel of heroin wrapped in a condom. She bent over and kissed me, passing it from her mouth to mine. It was quick. I looked left and she looked right.

The alarms went off about three feet from our table. A door burst open, and five or six officers charged toward our table and pounced on Jenny and me. One officer pinned me to the floor and had his hands around my throat to try to keep me from swallowing the package. I was dragged out of the visitor section, kicking and choking, desperately trying to swallow, which I eventually managed to do.

I was dragged to the block. An officer on each arm and one on each leg carried me into the cell, pinned me to the floor, cut my clothes with scissors, and pulled them off to see if I had any drugs on me. They knew I had swallowed them, so I was charged with smuggling and given twenty-eight days to add to my sentence. I was also put on closed visits, which meant no contact with anyone without a screen between us.

Month later my crown court date finally came through to be sentenced. Since I was pleading not guilty on some of my charges, I had spent a lot of time trying to study my depositions to prepare for court. One particular undercover detective had joined the long list of detectives who had vowed to lock me up for a very long time. I knew that day I would face both him and a jury.

The atmosphere on the journey to court was tense. Some were expecting very long sentences, some a life sentence. I saw my barrister and he told me it wasn't looking good because the police had eyewitnesses who were ready to testify. I knew I was guilty, but it was up to them to prove it.

Even though I tried anything I could to escape the sentence, it took the jury only one hour to find me guilty; it was unanimous. Once again, I was told I was a menace to society before being given a three-and-a-half-year prison sentence. Since I was told to expect up to five years, I was thankful of my sentence. Now I would be shipped out to a different prison.

Chapter 27

Shipped to Ranby

Weeks later, I was in a prison van heading three hours down the motorway to a new prison, HMP Ranby. It was a working prison, so no more twenty-three-hour days locked in a cell. In this prison I could wear my own trainers. I immediately hooked up with old acquaintances from previous sentences or old cellmates, who filled me in on who had what and what the score was.

Each of us was assigned to a wing and escorted there. The wing was a corridor with cells on either side, a TV room, and a dead end. To my surprise, each evening the gate at the end of the landing was locked, and we were left unlocked and able to move around from cell to cell. This was new to me. No more swinging lines to pass things from cell to cell.

We hung out, playing cards, drinking tea, and telling stories of past crimes. However, as I found out the hard way, if I were to have a fight with someone, no one was there to break it up. Bullying was rife. Personal belongings were demanded from the weaker ones who wouldn't put up a fight.

Anyone getting released the next morning would be pinned down, cursing and screaming, and carried by force to the end prison gate. His hands and legs would be spread out and tied firmly to the gate. Buckets of freezing cold water would be thrown over them, and sometimes eyebrows would be shaved off for a bit of fun.

The officers would occasionally come and see what all the screaming was about, see a lad tied up, and simply say, "Clean up after yourselves when you're done." Some lads took it in stride. Others would plead the day before to be moved off the wing to escape the affair. We always cleaned up as cell inspections were every Saturday morning.

Saturday morning would be manic cleaning before the shout of "Stand by your beds! Inspection!" White gloves were worn. If my cell was dirty, I would be punished, not only by officers, but also the inmates and branded a scruff. After a couple of weeks, I was moved to another wing, having been given a job gardening around the prison. I was amazed at just how much drug dealing was going on. Little gangs of lads here and there were selling various drugs: weed, heroin, tablets.

Apparently, I had been moved onto the wing that was the main source of supply to the prison. For just a ten-pound wrap of heroin, I could have my face totally slashed open by a total stranger wanting to get high.

The day was coming to an end. It was bang up. I would finally meet my new cellmates. It was a good night. I made new friendships with Yorkshire men, like myself.

The next morning, I started my new job in the prison gardens and was showed the ropes and the little scams they had going. The prison had two thousand chickens, and eggs were stolen and smuggled by the dozen onto the landings and hidden for night-time supper. As soon as the prison officers had done their final head count and the gate was locked for the night, the spliffs would come out and eggs would be prepared for munchies later. Someone would steal a metal meal tray for us, and we would scramble the eggs and cook them on the tray with cotton sheets burning underneath it.

Weeks passed, and it seemed I had earned trust, so I was given drugs to deal in exchange for tobacco, gold rings or chains, phone cards, and food. Now and again the wing we were all on would be raided by a posse of prison officers tipping up beds, pulling out drawers, and ransacking the whole place, searching for evidence of drug dealing. If they found anything, the person under suspicion would be moved to the segregation block and then shipped to another prison. We call it the "Ghost Train." They didn't usually find anything as we all had lumps plugged inside us.

A tattooist had recently turned up in the jail and was doing tattoos in exchange for drugs. While he was tattooing, someone would keep watch and play loud music to drown out the sound of the tattoo gun buzzing. We decided to make our own tattoo gun for our own wing to tattoo at night. We smashed an old radio; removed the motor from the tape recorder; stole sewing machine needles and Indian ink from art class; bent a spoon to rest the motor; and, with a bit of creativity, glue, and tape, made a working tattoo gun, which we wired into the electrical socket to turn the mini motor. It worked like a dream.

We tattooed each other most nights and made a complete mess of one another. We were obviously not professionals; nevertheless, we carried on. My head, knees, back, legs, and arms were tattooed with devils and skulls, which are still there to this day. All of us ended up with some very bad tattoos, which I am sure we wished we'd never done.

Chapter 28

Out of Prison and Out of Control

Another Christmas passed quickly. As the New Year began, I felt as though my mind was out of control. It was sick and evil. I didn't feel safe with my own thoughts or comfortable in my own skin. I didn't know who I really was or whether I had any purpose in this life, and I hadn't achieved anything; I had just left a trail of destruction behind me. I was told I would never achieve anything and that one day I would end up doing a life sentence for murder. I believed it and accepted that as the path I had chosen. There was no other.

Prison didn't seem to be a punishment. It became more of a second home. I don't say this in an arrogant way; I was institutionalised and enjoyed the banter and friendships I made in prison. It was a place where I recovered from addiction and planned future raids and robberies before doing it all again. Most of the time the police caught me on the streets. I was usually almost dead through endless abuse to my veins and my entire body.

By the time I was released, I had built up enough strength to do it all again. I wasn't interested in giving up drugs or getting clean. They hid all the pain I had buried over the years, and I was scared to dig it up, deal with it, and discover the real me.

I always felt alone in the world. My family was all broken up and didn't function like a family apart from my gran the legend and my aunty Cheryl. Without the crime and the drugs, there was nothing left. I was an empty shell that didn't know how to function in life.

My time in prison was coming to an end. It felt as if it had been a long time since I tasted freedom. If it hadn't been for my gran and my aunt offering me a place to stay, I would have been homeless when I got out. My gran and my aunt were the only two people in my family who meant anything to me; they were my rock. I didn't see them very often, but I knew they really cared about me. I always knew they were there for me.

The weeks turned into days, and I was on my final countdown to being released from prison. The night before my release I shaved my head and had it tattooed, as though I was sticking two fingers up at the system and the world. In the morning my head was still bleeding and swollen. My clothes stank because they had been in a box on a shelf for a very long time. I wasn't a pretty sight. I wondered if I was going to be released or kept in for breaking prison rules. But they were keen to get rid of me. The prison gates opened, and I was free.

It felt both good and strange to be free. The noise, the smells, the busy road, everyone was rushing around everywhere. No bars, no jangling keys, no officers calling my name, it felt good to be free. The first night I managed to stay in with my gran and my aunt. I promised them I had changed, but I found my way back to Brooklyn the next day, cooking up heroin on a dirty spoon with old friends and ready to shoot up again. They quickly filled me in on who had died from heroin overdoses since I had been away and who was currently dealing.

That night I returned completely smashed to my gran's. I felt so guilty I had let her and my aunt down. I was slipping back into my old ways fast, and soon my arms and legs were bruised and full of needle holes. My gran was getting upset and I couldn't understand why I would do this to her. I broke down in tears for the first time in many years and showed her my arms, apologising. My aunt Cheryl, who was a nurse, was visiting gran at the time and invited me to stay with her in Leeds, miles away from the area, so I could try to withdraw from heroin. I was thankful for the help.

During the day, while she was at work, I would be home alone, trying to sweat it out. In an effort to take my mind off withdrawing, I would walk around the area, looking for a suitable house to burgle, or a car to steal. Despite her genuine love for me, the pull of the drug was too much, and without warning I left sweating and full of cramps and pain back to Brooklyn where I found an old mate who was happy to share his gear. He told me he had attacked a drug dealer the week before and was planning attack that day.

That was the way it was going now. People were using violence to get what they needed. Anything could happen, and things could get very nasty. I volunteered to go with him, so we armed ourselves with hammers, made our way to his place, and did what we had to do. Later we got high and reminisced on old times.

I lived in an area where I had to be on the lookout all the time. There were contracts out on me and armed gangs looking for me, hungry for blood and revenge. One night I was chatting with a neighbour on the top floor landing of a block of flats when I looked out of the window, and in the distance, in the middle of the road, coming toward the block was about fifteen lads, all armed and fanned out across the street. It was dusk and I could see the shapes of the weapons in their hands shinning off the streetlights. They were carrying bats and knives.

I was caught off guard instantly and knew they were looking for me. I had no weapons on me and no one to fight with me, so I had to move fast. I went down the fire escape at the back of the flats and scrambled down the stairs. I ran into the basement where the residents' sheds were, which was a mistake. It was a long corridor that dead ended into a brick wall; it had nine sheds in it.

I darted inside and found a shed that was unlocked. I wedged my back against the door with my feet against the wall. My heart was pounding. *What a stupid place to hide,* I thought to myself. If anything had happened, no one would have seen or heard anything. I heard some of the lads shouting to one another, "He couldn't have gone far! Find him! I swear I am going to kill him! I am serious; he is a dead man!" They came into the sheds, banging the doors one by one as they came toward me. I was cornered. If they found me, I would be cut to pieces dead for sure.

Then a voice came and shouted, "Leave it! He's not here! He must have run down toward the river!" So, they ran toward the river. I knew I had just escaped my death. Sometimes I was the hunter, but that day I was the hunted. It was a crazy lifestyle, but I could see no way out. I had planned my escape route and made it out alive.

A couple of weeks later, in broad daylight, on a busy street, a car skidded up outside the house where I was staying, and five men wearing black balaclavas ran at the front door of the house I was in and began to chop it down with axes. I had no chance against them. Again, I could see the axes coming through the door from the inside. Again, I thought it was the end of my life but decided I wouldn't go without a fight.

Just before the door looked as though it was going to come down, some cars came up the street and someone screamed. The axemen ran off quickly; it was another close one.

Things were getting on top of me. I had broken my prison licence yet again. I had lost count of the crimes I had committed, and my crack and heroin habits were getting bigger, and the crimes were more serious than they'd ever been. I went to see a friend, who was a car dealer, about a second-hand car. He would give me a car on the promise that I would pay for it with gold, cash, or other stolen goods. The car got me out of the area to commit further crimes in other places.

One of my mates was a bit nuts; he loved to fight. I could always count on his backup when needed. He loved to play chicken with his knife. I was not allowed to move while he threw his knife at my feet. It usually stuck in the floorboards way too close to my feet, and then I would take my turn. We would play until we got injured or bored.

After having been released only a few months earlier, things were already going from bad to worse. Friends who had been recently arrested told me the police were asking questions about where I was hanging out, so I knew they were already on my case.

I had recently been in a violent fight in the Brooklyn area and needed to get away until things calmed down. Taking a huge supply of methadone to withdraw from heroin, I found a bed and breakfast miles away in Huddersfield. There were other lads in the same place injecting speed, so I would swap my methadone for speed, which would keep us up for two or three days without any sleep.

The supply was running out, and money was needed, so the only answer was to commit more crime to pay for the drugs. With no clean needles around, I would sometimes have to dig into the dirty needle bucket and rinse someone else's needle out to use. Some had to sharpen theirs by scraping them against a brick wall. It was gruesome, but at the time it made sense.

Chapter 29

Back to Prison

I had only been in Huddersfield a month and was arrested for handling stolen goods. I was bailed to appear in court where months later I was given twelve months to attend a Drug Offender Support Programme. I agreed to go, but I had no intention of going and left Huddersfield to return to Brooklyn. Once again, nothing had changed.

Back in Bradford, heroin and crack cocaine were now at an all-time high. There was a lot of bloodshed, turf wars, and taxing. Taxing was when people ganged together, armed with machetes or guns, and kicked in drug dealers' doors, demanding each other's drugs at gun point or knife point. One guy had a kettle full of boiling water and threatened to pour it out over someone's bare feet to make him surrender his stash of drugs.

Having skipped bail and failing to appear at the drug centre, the inevitable happened again. In the early hours of the morning, the police kicked down the door, and I was arrested again. As usual, I was stripped of my clothes and given a thin white paper suit to wear, as my clothes were all sent to forensics to see if they could find anything. I was locked down for forty-eight hours in the police cells and grilled about local crimes. I said nothing and was out yet again before awaiting a new sentence.

The prison doctor lived up to his name, Dr No, and I found myself locked in a cell with a total stranger and nothing to take the edge off my withdrawal.

A few weeks went by, and I was shipped to another prison to serve out my sentence. Within months, I had landed a prized job as a kitchen worker, making meals for the prison. I concentrated a lot of my efforts on stealing small amounts of yeast and fruit to make homebrew and sell it to other inmates. We hid our homebrew in the roof where the sniffer dogs couldn't smell it out. Occasionally cells were searched, and people busted, but it was all part of the game.

Before I got arrested, I had been spending a lot of time with people who were into dream interpretation and tarot cards. The subject fascinated me, and I passed many long hours in my cell, reading books on the supernatural, devils, and witches. A friend gave me a book to read, which clearly shouldn't have been in prison. It was called the Necronomicon, and it was all about demons and their ranks, each having different powers and seals, and how to perform rituals with blood, mirrors, and other stuff.

As I read it, part of me knew something was very wrong about this book. I felt uneasy reading it, though I could sense it was a dangerous and mysterious book. The lad who gave it to me had a small altar in his cell, which he kept a bowl of his blood on. He never stopped playing thrash metal and was a very confused and angry lad. Now I know why.

The sentence passed very slowly. I decided that when I was released, I would move to Leeds to try to make a clean start away from the drug scene. I was sick of my addictions. My life seemed to go round in circles. I was depressed, but no one would have known. As far as everyone around me was concerned, I was a happy-go-lucky guy. I realised I was wearing a mask to hide the real me because I was afraid of the person underneath who really wanted to change.

I would always be daydreaming about what could have been. I was tormented by "if only's": "If only I had done better at school," If only I had got on with my family," If only…." Everyone who knew me thought I was a psycho, a criminal, and a drug addict involved in gangs. I desperately wanted to give myself a chance, so I decided to move to Leeds on my release.

Chapter 30
Another Crime Spree

The release date came round quick, and I was given twenty-eight pounds discharge grant and sent on my way. I was given some help to find a bedsit. It was smaller than my prison cell and very grim. Indeed within a few days I began to bump into old cellmates from HMP Armley who lived in the Leeds area. All were crackheads and all were too keen to share.

Still on license from prison, within weeks I began another crime spree, stealing cars to use for house and factory burglaries. All the money went straight into the crack pipe, and any money left over I shot up my arm in the form of heroin. I had wasted away and lost control again. I was soon caught after about six months. I was pale, skinny, and full of holes.

After reoffending so soon, I knew I was going to get stung with another big sentence. I was right. The judge gave three years and ten months, which was three months more than my last sentence. I didn't know it at that point, but that was to be my final prison sentence.

HMP Armley hadn't changed one bit. I knew I was going to have a massive cold turkey. By the time I arrived, I already had the cramps and was starting to sweat and feel sick. I didn't sleep at all that night. I was in serious pain, pacing up and down, alternating between hot and cold sweats, and now I was hallucinating. But I survived until the morning, feeling very desperate.

Our door opened for one hours exercise. Immediately I found an old burgling friend from my area. He had been in only two days for a smash and grab on a jeweller's shop. He looked rough and was also withdrawing. I asked if he had anything to trade, and to my surprise he still had a diamond ring, which he had hidden in his body. After much persuasion, he trusted me to trade it later that day. The ring had gone and both of us had bags of heroin put under our door by prisoner cleaners.

The weeks turned into months. I knew I was going to serve even more years. My thoughts often turned to suicide, but I never gave into it. For years I had taken prison in my stride, but now watching the years slip by, I needed to change. I hated myself. I always wondered what it would be like to have a normal family and a normal job and be a good father to my children.

My date to be sentenced came. Handcuffed and taken up to face the judge, I gave the usual attitude, was told I was a menace to society, and given three years and ten months to serve.

There was a battle going on inside me. Part of me knew I needed to change. My drug addictions were getting bigger and more expensive, the crimes were getting more serious, and the sentences were getting longer. Most of my life had been spent in custody. Another part of me seemed to be at war with the idea that there was a battle going on within me. I would hear a voice telling me that change was for weak people, and it would never happen.

I was settling into my sentence, and a couple of lads I had known for years started talking about a new prison in Devon, almost three hundred miles away. They said it ran as a drug therapy programme, and most attractive of all were rumours that there were TVs in the cells. We laughed our socks off at the thought of a TV in a cell. We had known only hardcore prison twenty-three hours a day in a cell with a bucket. I didn't know if it was a windup or not, but what if it were true?

The next morning when my cell door was unlocked, I decided to go to the prison staff office and ask about it. To my surprise, it really did exist, but because it was so far away, not many had been accepted. I walked away with the address in my pocket. At this point I had no intention of seeking any therapy or genuine help. I was just looking for an easy ride for the rest of my sentence.

That night in my prison cell, I wrote to the Therapy Unit to plead for help with my addictions. It was a heart's cry, but I was half joking and half serious. The next day I posted the letter and forgot all about it.

I never expected a reply.

Chapter 31

Heading to the Therapy Unit

The months passed slowly. Finally, I received a letter back from the Therapy Unit. I couldn't believe it: they had accepted me. The unit was located in HMP Channing's wood in Newton Abbot, North Devon, and the letter said that arrangements were being made to transport me and other prisoners sometime soon. Soon turned out to be a month later, and I and a few others were handcuffed to each other and placed on a prison coach for the long journey. We stopped halfway there and stayed in HMP Bristol for the night.

The next morning, after our sloppy warm porridge and a few quick searches, we hit the road again. The roads soon turned to winding country lanes, and after a couple of hours the prison came into view. From the outside, it looked just like any other prison: gloomy with high walls, razor wire, and dogs patrolling. I began to wonder what I had let myself in for.

Coming off the coach we were greeted with a smile and unusually friendly prison officers. I was freaking out. It all felt weird and uncomfortable.

Once inside the wall, we were uncuffed and taken to reception to be booked in and to receive our bed packs. The therapeutic community (TC) was a prison within the prison, separated from the main prison. The guys in main prison didn't seem to like those of us in the therapy unit, evidenced by the lads who gave us our bed packs in reception.

We were soon picked up by two friendly officers from the TC, who took us to the unit. The gate was opened and in we walked. There were a few prisoners about. They wore neatly ironed shirts, they were clean shaven, and all of them had the same stupid smile on their faces. *What is it with these people?* I wondered. *Have they forgotten where they are?* Each of them was wearing a brightly coloured badge with a level and their name.

Once in, we were taken to the office and introduced to the staff. To my surprise they wore their own clothes and were ex addicts. We were then introduced to two prisoners who were the coordinators of the community. Apparently, the prisoners ran the unit while the prison staff took a back seat and watched the coordinators who were near the end of their programme run. To top it off, there was no TV in my cell. It was not a good day.

Later that evening, I was taken to the office to sign a contract that said I would abide by all the rules. I signed it begrudgingly. I found some guys I had known from Bradford who had been there a while. They filled me in, but they were different. Something about them had changed, and they were serious about change.

It was called a self-help community, which meant if there was a problem with someone's behaviour or attitude, the others in the community would point it out to that person. If the person took it well, fine. But if the person took it negatively, he would be taken to an encounter group during the week, which is a circle of people from the unit challenging that person on his behaviour or attitude. If he accepted their challenge, apologized, and promised to work on the behaviour, good, but if not, his name would be logged in a book, and he would be given a warning to be kicked off and sent back to another mainstream prison.

That same evening, I had to attend a meeting run by prisoners. There were about eighty men in total and the two coordinators stood at the front. I had to stand to my feet and be officially welcomed. The whole room started clapping. At that moment I was embarrassed and thought I had been tricked and sent to the funny farm for mad people. I was called out and given a nice shiny badge with my name on it. Whoop, whoop! I was officially crazy.

In the same meeting, people were called to the front and given different badges, which meant they had moved to a higher level and therefore received more responsibility. That evening in my cell alone, I began thinking of ways to get out of there, maybe cause a riot or a fight, punch the staff.... I just wasn't sure if I wanted to change.

But I gradually found myself getting used to the place, and over the next few weeks I made some good friends. The staff were ok once I got used to them, but the other prisoners were constantly telling me off for my attitude and aggressive behaviour.

Chapter 32
Discovering the Drug-Free Me

So, two weeks running, I found myself in an encounter group because of my behaviour challenges. Did I have an attitude? Yes, absolutely. I refused to shave, iron my clothes, clean my room, and mop the corridors. I gave everyone the same two-finger salute. My behaviour had not gone unnoticed, and I was soon called to the main office. After been given a good telling off, I was given my final ultimatum: either I accepted the community rules and committed to change, or I would leave on the next van back to a dirty Yorkshire prison and go back on twenty-three-hour lockdown. I realised they were serious, so I promised I would give it my best shot.

One of the things I had to do on the community was write my life story, stand before everyone, and read it out loud. It was a big deal for all of us. I had spent my whole life as a criminal who used drugs to hide the real pain. So digging up the past and finally facing the reality of how grim it had really been was a tough task for me. But when I listened to other people share their life stories, I realized that many of them were similar to mine. I began to realise I wasn't the only one who'd had a rough deal in the world and who felt angry and abandoned. At that point, I began to chill out.

Each morning and evening the whole community gathered in a room to listen to someone read aloud the philosophy and community rules we were to live by. Change took a while for me, but the others were patient. I was on an emotional rollercoaster ride. I felt unmasked and exposed as I tried to come to terms with getting to know the real me.

As the months went by, I started enjoying the process of discovering the real drug-free me. Gradually I was given responsibilities in the unit and was a hundred precent committed to change. After two years, I was offered the role of community coordinator, which I accepted. It was the first time I had ever achieved anything and been trusted with any responsibility.

As coordinator, I would meet with staff members to discuss each day and the progress of different individuals in the community. The coordinators would take the morning and evening meetings, delegate work, carry out job appraisals, and organise reports.

Chapter 33

Matty, the God Squad

Over the two years I spent in the community, I made some genuine friends. One was Matthew. Matty was a chunky lad from Manchester, and he was in for drug offences. He laughed like a hyena and reminded me of Popeye the sailor. We got on and hung out together daily.

Even though Matty was a good lad, he belonged to the God squad. He had a Bible in his cell and was always banging on about Jesus and church. I felt sorry for him because I thought some preacher had brainwashed him. I would constantly wind him up about his faith, but it didn't seem to bother him. The truth is I'd had many Bibles in prison over the years, but I never read them. The prison Bible pages were so thin that they made great cigarette rolling papers, so I must have smoked Mathew, Mark, Luke, and John. Many inmates did the same, but I didn't tell Matt.

We were in the last stages of the programme, which meant moving from a single cell into a double cell with someone. Matthew and I moved into a double cell together. I had the top bunk, and he had the bottom. Most nights he let me know when he was about to pray and asked me if I wanted prayer for anything. I didn't understand it, but to be polite, I would say, "Pray for me."

I could always hear him. He would often pray in a funny language. I recognised it to be the sound I heard many years earlier when I tried to take my own life. I didn't tell Matty it sounded like he was malfunctioning. I was worried for him. It was a bit weird, but he seemed pleased about it, so I let him crack on with it.

One Sunday, he asked me to go along with him to church. I had only ever been to church through the roof so I could steal the safe. After I thought about it, I concluded, *What did I have to lose?* So, I agreed. I was never into God, just loads of dark, weird stuff. I had used the name Jesus many times but only as a swear word.

Sunday soon came around. Matty was excited. We got ready and waited for our cell door to be unlocked and were escorted to the prison church. I was greeted with a firm handshake and a smile and ushered into the chapel. It smelt a bit funny. I didn't know what to expect. When I was a kid, I had seen people going into church, but it never made any sense. Walking through the graveyard to meet a total stranger dressed like Darth Vader in a large, black robe, welcoming me into his spooky building was a scary thing for me. But this looked different. We sang a few old, strange songs about going to some river ("Take Me to the River") and another about some wonderful working power in the blood of a lamb. Although the songs made no sense to me, I was enjoying being out of my cell.

The preacher man got up and began to speak. Little did I know this man was to become a great inspiration to me and a lifelong friend. While he was speaking, I tried to tune him out. Part of me wanted to listen, but another part of me didn't. It was like some weird, invisible battle going on inside my head.

That evening back at the cell, Matt asked me what I thought about the service. He was stoked. I went along. I tried to make a joke about it, telling him I wasn't ready for sandals and socks and a huge Bible just yet. He went on to talk about being born again and having a clean slate and a fresh start in life through faith in Jesus. I didn't really understand it, but if such a thing really was possible, it sounded like I needed some of this Jesus.

I put my name down to be unlocked for church on Sunday.

Chapter 34

Coming to Know Jesus Christ

Sunday came round again. I knew what to expect this time. The chaplain remembered my name, and as the service started, I began to sing quietly. I wasn't so bad after all. Bill, the preacher, got up and began to speak. Again, it felt as though he was speaking directly to me. He was talking about making a fresh start in life with a clean slate by receiving forgiveness for everything I had ever done through Jesus. He said, "We have all fallen short of God's standard. We have all messed up at some point in life." Then he continued with, "We have all sinned against God, and that sin separates us from God."

I listened intently. Then he said something that blew my mind. He said, "God desires a relationship with us all and loves us, so he sent his only son, Jesus, to the earth to help make that possible. God sent Jesus, his one and only son, to bridge the gap that keeps us from having a relationship with God. Jesus gave his life for us. He was nailed upon a cross as a living sacrifice, and through the shedding of his blood, there is hope for us all to be free from guilt, shame, and sin."

Something was happening to me. My heart was pounding. I began to feel uncomfortable and excited at the same time. He continued to preach that, "When Jesus died upon that cross, it was not the end of the story, as the grave could not hold him. And three days later, he rose again in victory in resurrection power, which means Jesus made a way for us all to come into a personal relationship with God."

Wow! My heart was beating faster. Bill then told us that not only would our sins be forgiven through believing in Jesus, but the same spirit who raised Jesus from the dead, the Holy Spirit, wants to baptise us, come live in our hearts, and help us live godly lives.

Bill preached that we should "all open our hearts to receive Jesus and ask God for his forgiveness today."

He preached that God is faithful, that his grace is sufficient, that our slates would be wiped clean, and that our sins would be washed away forever. I was beginning to understand the reality of this message and the possibility of being forgiven and receiving God's peace. I knew God was on my case.

My hard, cold heart toward God was melting within me. I thanked Bill, and after the service he told me that Jesus didn't come to bring a new religion to the world. He came to die upon a cross to offer relationship.

Before I left the chapel that day and headed back to the main prison wings, Bill gave me a sheet with a prayer on it about how to ask God into my life. I stuffed it in my pocket.

Coming through the doors back to the wing, the other

lads were shouting, "Hey, over here, the God squad. Hey, Mark, you seen the light yet?" They were joking, and I could handle it. But something was stirring within me.

I couldn't get it out of my head. *What if it was true? What if I could be forgiven and have a clean slate and a fresh start in life?* I had always felt I had a huge hole inside me, a huge hole of emptiness that I could never fill. Girls couldn't fill it; drugs couldn't fill it; my fascination with the occult couldn't fill it; nothing could fill it. So many times over the years I had laid for hours and hours on my prison bed, dreaming of living a life without drugs, crime, and violence, and living a normal life with a loving family, being happy. A new life through Jesus means the dream really is possible.

Eventually the day came to an end, and I was relieved to be locked in my cell for the night. I waited for every cell door to be locked. I could hear them slamming shut, same old routine. When the last door slammed shut, I heard the keys jangling in the distance.

As I slowly began to wind down, I thought again about Jesus. It triggered memories of movies I had seen over the years. In most of them there was always a battle between good and evil, darkness and light. The good always won the battle in the end.

I began to realise that for many years I had been caught up in a battle between good and evil, between God and the devil. I had danced with devil and been deceived. I was overwhelmed with emotion as I began to realise God had been trying to get my attention to show me his love. I thought about what I had heard at the prison chapel and pictured Jesus hanging on the cross for me.

I waited for Matty to go to sleep. I got out of my prison

bunk and knelt on the floor and prayed. I asked God to forgive me for all the sin in my life and told him I needed Jesus to help me change. I thanked Jesus for dying on the cross for me and asked him to come into my life. I didn't know what to expect. There were no clashes of lightning or rolling thunder.

I suddenly felt an overwhelming, unexplainable peace come over me. I didn't understand what was happening, but I knew it was good. So, for a few moments I lingered in the warm, tingly peace, and suddenly happy tears began to run down my face. I had not cried for many years. These were not tears of pain; they were tears of relief that I had finally found freedom.

I felt love and an unexplainable peace overwhelm me, and I knew it was God. He had answered my prayer. I sensed a whispering voice of reassurance that everything was going to be ok, that I was safe. I stayed there a while, whispering "Thank you, God; thank you, God." Then, after some time, I slipped into bed to have what was one of the most peaceful sleeps I could ever remember.

Chapter 35

My New Identity in Christ

The next morning, as soon as I opened my eyes, I knew something had changed. For one I had never slept so well. I jumped out of bed, feeling free, fresh, and happy. I told Matty what had happened, and we praised God together. I felt as if a great weight had been lifted off me.

As I opened the curtains, I was greeted with a beautiful day. As I looked at the trees, birds, and flowers, I realised it was the first time I had really seen their beauty. I remembered what the prison chaplain had told me Jesus said in the Bible: "You will know the truth and the truth set you free." It was true. I believed and received God's love and forgiveness. God's truth had set me free from the weight of guilt, sin, and shame forever.

Soon afterward the cell door opened, and the day started. That day I told a few people I had given my life to Jesus. Given my background as a joker, not many people believed I was serious. In fact, most people thought I had finally lost the plot. Some shook my hand; others shook their heads.

Sunday came round fast. I gave Martin, the chaplain, the great news that I had accepted Jesus into my life, and we prayed and praised God. After the service he gave me a pocket-sized Gideon Bible and explained how to read it. When I got back to the Therapy Unit, I hid my Bible under my pillow in my cell, excited that I could read it later. I had only two weeks of therapy left before I would be moved to a new cell on a working wing to get a job in the prison.

That evening, after the usual mad, last-minute rush of everyone swapping newspapers and magazines to read when we were locked in our cells, I waited for Matty to go to sleep. The moment I had been looking forward to had finally come. I opened my Bible for the first time to start reading it, and immediately something strange happened. Inside my head, I experienced a rush of angry thoughts blaspheming God that were so strong they were shouting "Lies! Lies!" inside my head.

I opened the Bible. At the beginning on the left was a list of words to look up for encouragement. At the top of that list was the word *afraid*. Next to it was my name, *Mark*, and a reference (Mark 5:1). When I looked it up, I found a true story about a violent man possessed by evil spirits. He caused chaos in his community, and they rejected him. They would often bind him with chains and drag him to the graveyard where he was left alone. But he would often break the chains and run back into the community only to be bound and put back in the graveyard all over again. Left amongst the dead, he would cry out for help and cut himself with sharp stones.

But one day Jesus arrived in the place where he was. When Jesus stepped of the boat, the man ran to Jesus and fell at his feet. Jesus cast all the demons out of his life, and he was instantly and completely transformed, healed, and restored. Then Jesus told him to go back into the village where he had come from and tell them the great things God had done for him. The Bible says he went not only to his community, but five more surrounding communities, and they all marvelled when they saw him completely healed and transformed.

This story resonated within my heart, and I felt God was showing me that my life had been similar to this demon-possessed man. Just like him, I had been rejected and cried out for help. And like the demon-possessed man, when I opened my heart to Jesus, he healed me and radically transformed my life. Like this man one day I will also have an opportunity to go into the world and testify about what God has done in my life. I felt encouraged, strengthened, and for the first time, I felt excited about the future ahead. Everything was going to be ok.

I quickly began to realize that God speaks through his word, and I had such a hunger to hear from him.

The more I read the Bible, the more I get to know who God is. He is a living, loving God, who is patient, forgiving, and faithful. He is for me, not against me. For years I thought God was just an angry God who demanded we follow his rules, or we go to hell. Reading the Bible, however, I find that is not true. God has always loved me and everyone else, as well. And God says in his word that is it impossible for him to lie.

I believe every promise in the Bible, one of which is that even when I was still being formed in my mother's wombs God had a plan and a purpose for my life. He has always loved me with an everlasting love, and he is as faithful as the air we breathe. I know with every part of my being that I really do have a clean slate and a fresh start. The old life is gone a new one has begun.

A new life in Jesus means I have a whole new identity, a kingdom identity. I am no longer a slave to sin. I am now the son of a king. When I began to understand how God saw me it also changed my perspective on how I saw people. The Bible says that when we surrender to God, we are like a piece of old clay in God's hands. He begins to mould us and shape us into the people he intends us to become. God began to shape my thoughts and helped renew my mind and see myself as he sees me. God sees our potential, not as we are, but as we will be when we connect to his plans and purposes.

Chapter 36
Leading Others to Christ

As the weeks rolled into months, my thoughts and my attitudes toward everyone around me began to change as God was shaping and moulding my character. For the first time, I finally felt comfortable in my own skin. I could ditch the mask and be who I was destined to be.

By now the men on the wing were seeing a huge change in me and would often say, "You've changed since you've joined the God squad." The lads would often come into my cell in the evenings during recreation time, push the door behind them, and ask me to pray for them and their children or loved ones.

I was still new to praying and still didn't know the correct way to pray, but the Bible says that if I opened my mouth God would fill it. So, I would open my mouth and believe God would fill it, and he always gave me the right words to pray and encourage others. The more time I spent reading the Bible and talking to God, the more I felt my faith grow. I stood for what I believed in with an unshakable faith.

I continued to pray that I would get the job at the prison chapel. After a few weeks I was overjoyed to hear that I had gotten it. God had answered my prayers, and I began working in the prison chapel. God was really moving in my life. I was hungry for the Bible and would often fall asleep with my head in it. I hang on every word that I read.

My job in the chapel was perfect: cleaning the toilets and preparing the chapel for Alpha classes and Bible studies. Through working in the chapel, I got to know the Rev. Bill Hill quite well. He was an amazing man. He really loved the prisoners, regardless of what they were in for. He wouldn't stand for any messing about, but he won the respect of everyone, whether they were Christians or not. He would lend guitars to inmates during their stay.

When he baptised people, he would use a dustbin. The person would get in the dustbin as a sign of cleansing the trash from their life. Then he would dunk them under it and empty it away. I developed a great friendship with Bill. I didn't know it then, but he was to become a lifelong friend.

After reading about baptism in the Bible, I made the decision to get baptised. A date was set for the baptism, and I invited the whole therapy community in the morning meeting. I thought only a few lads would come to the service, but about thirty men and even some of the officers came. It was an awesome day.

The wheely bin was waiting at the front of the church. For the first time I had to tell people why I had chosen to follow Jesus. I felt emotional, sick, and slightly shaky, but the presence of God filled the place. I sensed the same peace I had the first day. I knew God was right there with me.

I fumbled my way through my testimony. It was probably only one sentence long. My mouth was dry, and my body was shaking. I climbed into the wheely bin, and three buckets of water were poured over my head, one in the name of the Father, one in the name of the Son, and one in the name of the Holy Spirit.

I felt cleansed from the inside out, and I began to speak in a language I didn't understand. I couldn't seem to stop strange words from pouring out of my mouth. I was quickly wrapped in a towel, and I was reassured later that it was a prayer language, called tongues, that God had given me. Then I remembered my cellmate also prayed in this language. I spoke in the language for a long time and felt as though I was walking on air.

That day Matty rededicated his life to God and was baptized the same day in the same water. Over the next few months, I saw many others choose to follow Jesus and be baptised. Just like me, their lives were forever changed as God began to heal and restore them.

Chapter 37

New Life, New Friends, Drug-Free

The months seem to fly by quickly.

Finally, my time in prison was coming to an end, even though I had nowhere to go once I was released. I knew I couldn't go back to my old area in west Yorkshire. That would be like swimming with crocodiles. Everyone I had ever known was mixed up in the underworld; they were either criminals, drug addicts, psychos, or a combination of all of them.

I believe in the power of prayer, so I began to pray every day to move to Devon and to make a new start as a new creation away from the world of drugs and crime. I prayed that God would help me settle in a new community, find a job, and wife who has a fiery faith. I wanted a clean break in a new area, and I believed with all my heart that God could do it.

My release date was quickly approaching. I continued to pray each morning with Bill, and one day, out of the blue, God answered all my prayers in miraculous ways. It still blows my mind how God heard me and orchestrated every little detail. He is awesome! Not long before I was about to be released, a local retired Vicker, named Ted, and his wife, from Devon, started coming into the prison to lead a Tuesday-night Bible study. I connected with the couple, and we became friends.

After the Bible study we would talk and pray for one another. I told Ted about my situation and asked if he would pray for me during the week while he was at home. He agreed, but without me knowing, they had arranged to meet the prison governor to ask if I could be released to live with them at their Devon home. Ted was a retired minister of an Anglican church in the village. The governor agreed, and two days before Christmas I was released from the prison, with a small brown paper bag containing all my possessions and a huge smile on my face, and I moved to Devon.

The faithfulness of God is amazing; everything the Bible says is true. I had read a verse in the Bible that said to trust in the lord with all your heart and lean not on your own understanding; in all your ways acknowledge him and he will make your paths straight. Wow, God had answered my prayers as I trusted him.

I felt good to be free. My new home was off the beaten track, deep in the Devon countryside. I was living in a huge house with white cob walls and thatched roofs surrounded by rolling hills as far as the eye can see, with gardens full of sheep. It was an old rectory. I was given my own quarters at the other end of the house with a stunning view looking out the window.

Each morning we would meet around the piano in the huge drawing room to praise God, read the Bible, and pray. In the garden each day, I was set to work chopping down trees and mending fences. It felt good swinging the axe to chop logs in the sunshine and in the fresh country air.

Every day there was plenty of work to do. I felt so grateful to God that I was finally free and living outside a prison drug-free with zero desire to ever use again. I had no real bearing as to where I was in the world, other than knowing I was in Devon. At lunch break I would wander out of the gates of the rectory for an adventure across the road. There was a village church where I would often go and sit down in silence to pray.

On some occasions there would be a lady, called Julia, cleaning and arranging flowers. She was cheery, and she we would often say hello before she made her way out. Little did I know this was a divine setup from God, for in a few years' time, this lady was going to be my mother-in-law. God was preparing me to marry her daughter, who I had not even met yet. God has such a sense of humour.

Chapter 38

Sensing God's Presence

After a few months, I finally got my bearings and realised I was just a few miles from the city of Exeter. One morning I walked into the village and caught a bus there to look up Bill, the prison chaplain who had baptized me, as he had often spoken about his church in the centre of Exeter. I promised him before I left the prison that I would find him as soon as I was settled.

I soon found Riverside Christian Church, a place at the bottom of the city down by the river. It looked huge from the outside. I walked through the front doors, into the modern café area, and made my way to reception. I soon found Bill. We shook hands and praised God that we had found each other outside prison.

Bill showed me around. I had only known the small prison chapel, so this church, which was once a nightclub, was totally mind blowing to me. It had large halls, offices, youth rooms, conference rooms, and a café bar.

On our tour around, I met the pastor, John Partington. He was friendly, fun, and direct. Bill wasted no time inviting me to the Sunday morning service and arranged for someone who lived in the same village as I did to pick me up.

I will never forget that first Sunday service. It was packed with at least a couple hundred people. I had only sung hymns with piano accompaniment in the prison. I didn't know anything else. When the band got up and the music started, the place came alive. People were singing, dancing, cheering jumping up and down, and waving their arms about to the drums and electric guitars. This was a whole new experience for me, and I loved it. The place was electric with genuine joy and people praising God.

There was a moment in the service where a couple were called out to the front of the church. After they talked about going to Hillsong Bible School in Australia, people gathered around them to pray. Then the pastor and friends of the couple came forward to pray for them.

While they were praying, something happened to me. I was on the front row with Bill when I felt as though a bolt of lightning hit my body and stayed on me. I began shaking and biting my lips. It was like dropping a packet of mentos into a bottle of coca cola. Suddenly everything in me erupted and sweat began to drip from my chin. I felt like I was on fire, and for some reason I wanted to laugh out loud. I could barely hold it in.

Thankfully Bill could see I was a mess and reassured me I wasn't cracking up. He told me I was sensing the Holy Spirit and the presence of God. All my life I had risked my freedom, committing crimes to get money to get high and had every addiction under the sun. Yet that morning I experienced the greatest feeling ever, a lightning bolt of joyful liquid love. I have never been the same since that day and continue to spend time in God's presence daily.

Bill and I began to meet regularly when he wasn't on duty at the prison, and our friendship grew strong. I wanted to serve God and give something back to the world I had always taken everything from. I felt alive, free, thankful, and joyful that I could serve God and live a life free of chaos and addiction. There were always things to be done around the church, so I chatted with Bill about my desire to serve God wherever he needed help.

The next day I arrived early at the church, eager and grateful to God to start the day. After morning coffee with Bill before he headed off to work at the prison, he would set me up with the right tools and instructions. My first job was painting a few small rooms on the bottom floor. Every morning Bill would keep me supplied in fresh paint and brushes. Three weeks later I had painted all the floors.

Coming to church on Sunday and serving there throughout the day, I made new friendships, so when the staff and volunteers went home, they would leave me locked in. I usually let myself out, sometimes as late as midnight. I was so grateful to be alive and living a normal life; serving God was the icing on the cake.

On the weekends I loved attending the services where people would dance, sing, and have fun. I love the joy and enthusiasm the people had for God, especially the way they preached and gave me a better understanding of the Bible.

Chapter 39

A Doorkeeper in the House of God

One Monday morning I was painting the corridors. I hadn't been to church that Sunday as the person who lived in the same village as I did couldn't make it. I was always grateful for the lift and was praying that God would make a way for me to get to church without having to rely on others.

As I was painting and praying, Pastor John and Bill came to see me for a chat. Pastor John said, "Come with me. I want to show you something. We have an idea." He took me to a big room behind the stage at the back of the church hall. The room was large but dark and dirty and full of cobweb-covered boxes of old music equipment and tins of out-of-date food.

John enthusiastically came straight out with what he was thinking: "Why don't we build you a flat here? We will make a bedroom, plumb in a bathroom, and build a kitchen?" He continued with, "We can buff up the floor and put in some radiators and widows in. You can live in as our caretaker. What do you think?" I was overjoyed and accepted.

Almost straight away, we set to work clearing the rooms to make it happen. Bill, I, and other volunteers from the church built the flat, and three months later it was ready to move into. It looked amazing, and I moved in as the church caretaker. God had answered my second prayer in the prison that I would find a good job. Plus, I would never be late for church again. What a blessing to be a servant in the house of God.

As I was reading my Bible daily, God showed me a scripture about being a door keeper in the house of God. Wow! I realised in that moment just how much Jesus had radically changed my life forever. In the past, I would have dismantled the alarms system in the building and spend the early hours clearing out the office equipment and busting the safe. Yet because of Jesus, I had now been given the keys to the church to guard and protect everything in it.

Chapter 40
Restored Family Relationships

During the evenings I had plenty of time to think about my life. I know God had completely forgiven me and set me free for all the damage I had done in the world and to others. Yet I still felt I needed to contact my mother and my three daughters. I had not been in any of my daughters' lives at all and really wanted to ask for their forgiveness. I had completely failed to be a father and missed the best years of their lives.

I began to pray and ask the Holy Spirit to help me. I knew what I had to do. I wrote letters to my mother and then my daughters, asking them to forgive me for how I had lived my life and the hurt I had caused. I prayed over the letters before sending them out. The first letter was to my youngest daughter who lived with her grandmother. It was a tense wait for any reply.

The first response came via a private phone call to our pastor, warning him that he had a vicious thug, thief, and conman living in his church. He was told if he was wise, he would kick me out immediately. The pastor explained I was no longer the same person, and through God's grace, I had a compete transformation. He suggested they ring back in a few months to see how I was doing.

Thankfully they did ring back two months later and decided they had to see this for themselves. A date was arranged when they would travel to meet me. Needless to say, it was a hugely emotional but happy day. My daughter and I took a walk alone together during the day, and I asked her to forgive me. She forgave me, and we hugged for the first time. It was a very special day. Our relationship continues to grow stronger each day, and I am now a grandad.

Then something amazing happened. My eldest daughter made contact with me by letter. I hadn't seen her for sixteen years. We arranged to meet. I travelled to west Yorkshire, excited to see her. She was beautiful. It was another emotional but joyful day. I asked her to forgive me for being a terrible father and not being in her life, and she immediately forgave me. We cried, we laughed, and we hugged. Still today we have a healthy relationship, and she has given me two beautiful grandchildren.

Contact was made with my third daughter. She was as beautiful as the others. We met and I asked her to forgive me. She forgave me, and we began to rebuild our relationship. Today I have another two beautiful grandchildren.

I thank God for his amazing grace. The book of Joel tells us that God restores the years the locusts have eaten. God restored all my broken relationship with my daughters and with my mum.

Chapter 41
Speaking into Precious Lives

During one of my visits back to Yorkshire, the police found out I had been in the area and were told that I had changed and become a Christian. It must have been hard for them to believe at first, but after a while one CID officer, Mr Greenwood, who had been my archenemy, chased me all over Yorkshire and tracked me down. He made contact with me, saying he had heard I had become a Christian and that I had changed. He asked me if I would come back to Yorkshire to speak to a group of young first-time offenders.

I was very nervous about getting in touch with him. This man had once been my enemy. We had fought in the crown courts, me in the dock, speaking to the jury and fighting for my freedom, and Mr Greenwood in the dock, trying to put me away for a very long time. I eventually called him and arranged to go back to Yorkshire to speak to the lads.

Coming face to face was awkward at first, but we put the past behind us, and the day was a great success. I was able to inspire and encourage the young lads not to choose a life of drugs and crime.

On the drive home, I praised God and gave him all the glory for giving me the ability to speak into those precious lives. I knew from that moment that God would use me to speak to people struggling with addiction and a life of crime.

Chapter 42

Miracles in the Mission Field

Meanwhile it was a privilege to sit under John Partington's inspirational teaching and grow as a Christian. As the church caretaker, I was able to sit in on many meetings and conferences that took place in the building. This helped me grow in faith and feed my hunger for God.

After I had been in the church for about a year, the church decided to run a Bible school, called the School of Acts. It would provide people with solid biblical teaching and hands-on experience with evangelism, praying for the sick, and serving others. I knew it was the perfect next step for me to grow, and I wanted to enrol in the Bible school, but I had a problem. I had to come up with a large fee to enrol and I had no money.

Taking a step of faith, I asked God for the miracle of being able to attend Bible school. God made clear what I had to do. He's a miracle-working God. I enrolled in the school, and at the beginning of every month, Charlie

Ross, the dean of the school, would wave the envelope in front of the class, saying "Mark's monthly widow's mite." For the full duration of the Bible school, the cheques continued to come in as God supplied. I never saw one. I just kept turning up praise to God for his faithfulness.

I sat under Charlie Ross, and during school we went on a mission trip to Portugal. Our pastor, JP, came with us. The first day we relaxed after the flights and met our hosts. The next day, after prayer, we were put into groups of two. I was in a group with John, and it was a morning of street evangelism in the park, with the help of interpreters.

On one occasion John and I were walking through the park when a group of teens approached us. I was wearing shorts and a t-shirt, and they could see my head, arms, legs, and feet were covered in tattoos. They assumed I was a drug dealer and stopped us to see if they could buy drugs from us. Through an interpreter, I told them we didn't have any drugs, but we had something far greater than any drug: we have Jesus Christ. After sharing a short testimony, we sat down in the park and prayed. All of them received Jesus into their hearts as Lord and Saviour.

Through God encounters like these, my faith grew stronger and stronger.

That same day in the park, our mission team and the local church that was hosting us were due to hold an evangelistic event of worship and testimonies, but a wild bush fire was heading toward the park. As the park began to fill with smoke, the local mayor, who was there to welcome us and open the event, ran toward us, weeping. His friends needed help fast because the fire was heading toward their homes on the outskirts of town.

The pastor of the local church, the members of the church, the mayor, and I jumped in a car, and we followed close behind, driving through the smoke. After ten minutes, we came to a house in a clearing where a family from the church lived.

The fire could be seen in the distance, heading toward us. We all joined hands in a circle around the house and began to pray, some in English and some in Spanish, that the fire would not come near the home. After we had prayed for some time, suddenly the wind changed and the fire split. It looked as though it went round the house, but in the distance, we praised God.

Later, after the trip, when we arrived back in England, we were sent some ariel pictures of the house, and the fire had truly gone around it. The pictures showed a circle of black soot burnt into the ground around the home. What great memories of God answering the prayers of the people.

Upon our return, some friends from the church invited me to their house to testify about the trip. They only lived a few streets away from the church and gave me a key to come and go. It was a different space to relax in from time to time. The house was a shared house in which the owner, Jenny, lived with another girl. She said she had a spare room for someone to move into in the future. I didn't realise at the time that my future wife would be moving into it.

Chapter 43

Meeting My Wife

For a while, I had been asking God for a wife with a fiery passionate heart that would always put him first. God answered my prayer in a way that only God can when he wants to bring two people together to serve him.

Jenny and her housemate went to a Christian festival, called New Wine; it was like a mini-Glastonbury. People were camping in tents in fields and listening to Christian bands and speakers. During one of the meetings, my now-wife, Andrea, was worshipping when she sensed God tell her to speak to Jenny about a room.

When she approached Jenny, she politely tapped her on the shoulder and asked if she had a room to rent. It was a wow moment as they didn't know each other before then. Surprised, Jenny said, "yes," she had a room to rent in Exeter, and a date was set.

Andrea was living in the city of Bath at the time while she was finishing her doctorate at Bath University to become a clinical psychologist. Once she finished it, she moved into the spare room at Jenny's house just a few streets away from the church.

Andrea was born in Exeter and brought up in a village just a couple of miles away where her parents still live today.

When we first met, there was an instant attraction. I tried to play it cool, but I think it was obvious. Soon Andrea started coming to the church and we started hanging out together. But we hadn't talked about getting together.

Andrea soon got a job and a start date in Glastonbury. One day she asked me if I would like to come on a test run to her new job to time the journey before her first day of work. Of course, I said, "yes."

The test run turned out to be more than an hour's drive. We laughed and talked all the way. After the test run was complete, we began to make our way back, stopped at Glastonbury tour, and climbed a huge hill together with a three-hundred-and-sixty-degree view of miles and miles of countryside on a sunny day.

I will never forget that day. It was this day that Andrea told me that she felt God was pulling us together and that she felt love toward me. I told her I felt the same, but we needed to make sure it was God, so we decided we would not see each other for a week. Instead, both of us would pray see what God said to us individually. It was hard not seeing her, but I pressed in to seek God.

A week later we came together to share what God had been saying. As we began to share with each other, it was clear that God was speaking to us as he had given us the same scriptures. It was amazing. But we decided to separate one more time and pray once again. We separated and arranged to meet a few days later.

I remember being up my ladder painting a wall in my flat as I was praying about Andrea. I was asking God if he wanted us to come together, and I asked him to make it clear to me. I had not yet read the whole of the Old Testament, but God gave me a chapter and a verse to read. It was so loud and clear that I nearly fell of my ladder.

I picked up my Bible, wondering where this verse could be. I opened the Bible to start my search, and I opened it to a page I had never seen before, and my eyes were instantly drawn to a verse in the middle of the page. It was the story of a couple, Ruth and Boaz, who were attracted to each other and who God put together later in marriage. When Boaz woke up to find Ruth laying at his feet, instantly I knew that I would one day marry Andrea. Trying to play it cool, she said the same. God was putting us together.

Many years later, I was to find out that before we agreed to be married, Andrea had told her father she had already met her future husband. Andrea had just read a book by Yonggi Cho that advises people to be very specific in their prayers and write them down. So, she had written a detailed description of what her husband-to-be would be like.

She even prayed specifically about the colour of his eyes but couldn't decide whether she wanted her husband to have blue eyes or green eyes. When she met me and looked into my eyes for the first time, she realised God has a great sense of humour as I have one blue eye and one green eye. I guessed that answered her prayers.

Chapter 44

"Sylvester the Cat" Proposes to Andrea

After we had been dating for a while, I decided to propose to Andrea. Never to do things by halves, I came up with a crazy scheme to ask her to marry me. A friend of mine owned a horse. My plan was to hire a knight's costume, ride into the church hall during a meeting, and propose to her. I know JP would have been well up for it.

Unfortunately, or fortunately perhaps, depending on your viewpoint, the horse wasn't available the day I needed it, so I found myself at the fancy dress hire shop selecting an alternate outfit for the proposal. The only costume that would completely disguise me and deliver the desired surprise to Andrea was a Sylvester the cat outfit. I hired it, hid it away in the sound booth at the back of the church, and met JP to hatch the masterplan. John is always up for doing things outside the box and loves a good laugh, so this was going to be fun.

It was late December. If I was going to propose before the end of the year, it would have to be in our main Christmas Eve service. The stage was set. It was lights, camera, action. I went round to Andrea's to walk her to our Christmas service. It was a cold, frosty night. The church was lit up in Christmas lights, and the smell of freshly baked mince pies and coffee filled the air as we walked through the front doors of the church.

We walked up the stairs and into the main hall. It was filled with about 200 people. The ushers found us some seats, and the service began. JP would give me a secret signal for when I was to leave the main hall to get into the Sylvester the cat outfit. After a few carols and a short Christmas play by the kids, he gave me the signal. He told the children a very special guest was about to arrive and come to say hello. All the kids were shouting, "It's Santa Clause!"

I told Andrea I was popping to the toilet and slipped out of the service. A couple of minutes later, John announced it was time to welcome our special visitor. The Sylvester the cat theme tune was playing as I came in from the back of the hall, dressed as Sylvester. The kids were cheering, but most people were wondering what on earth was going on. John called Andrea to the front of the church. I took the costume's head off, got down on one furry knee, and proposed. Thankfully, she said, "yes."

We set a date for our wedding in four months' time and started planning it the next day. The time seemed to go slowly on the run up to the wedding. I joined a street team that went out at night from the church to carry hot soup to the homeless in doorways and tents. We often got to minister healing, shower them with love, and lead people to Jesus. I knew what Jesus had done for me and how opening my heart to him changed my life forever. For me to lead someone to Jesus was very exciting as I knew they were about to meet a living God who would love and protect them.

Chapter 45

Our Wedding

Our wedding day finally came. It was a time of great blessing and joy and a time to give thanks to God for his overwhelming goodness and provision. So many people blessed us in so many ways. Our pastor married us in our own church hall, and all our friends from the church dressed as waiters and waitresses and served the guests all day

On the big day, waiting as the music quietened, I turned to look down the aisle and saw the most beautiful woman I had ever seen. I sensed this was the beginning of many new adventures together. Once we said our vows, we danced down the aisle. For our honeymoon, we flew to Cancun, Mexico, and had an amazing time swimming with the dolphins and spending time together in the baking sun.

On our return from the honeymoon, Andrea and I both began to pray about the future and asked God how we could best serve him. We knew we wanted to get a house and have a baby, so we began looking for a place of our own.

Suddenly God began to answer our prayers as we began receiving invitations to testify. I was invited back into

HMP Channing Wood prison in Devon, the very same Therapy Unit I had been released from just a few years earlier. I was delighted and praised God. This was a great opportunity to inspire encourage and motivate those still trying to break free from addictions. I was invited into the daily meeting to testify to the men of what the power of God can do in a surrendered life. It was an unforgettable morning and one of many visits into the prisons.

Chapter 46

Miracles at Weston-Super-Mare

During our time at Riverside Church, Andrea and I became friends with another couple, Shane and Lorraine. We were in the same house group for some time. At that time Shane was JP's personal assistant. Riverside belongs to the Assemblies of God group of Pentecostal churches, and from time to time pastoral posts would come through the office, which Shane would pass on to others where appropriate.

Shane heard about a church in Weston-Super-Mare that needed a new pastor, and at first, he passed the details on to a few people he thought might be interested in the position. But the information kept landing back on his desk until he realized that God might be telling him he should take up the post himself. How that came to pass is a story in itself, but eventually, with encouragement from the pastor, he applied, got the job, and soon moved to Weston-Super-Mare. After he had been in the new post three or four months, he got in touch with us and asked us to pray about coming to assist him.

By that time Andrea and I had our own house, so joining Shane would be a massive step of faith. We decided to pray separately and come back together to see what God had said. After a few days of praying, God had said to both of us that we should go. As if to confirm our decision, we put our house on the market and it sold to a cash buyer within twenty-four hours. A few weeks later, we arrived in Weston-Super-Mare. After going through the interview process, I took on the role of assistant pastor.

We moved to Weston-Super-Mare and began to get a feel for the area. After we tried for some time, Andrea finally became pregnant with our first child. Both of us were excited to start a new adventure together and couldn't wait for the birth. We also wondered what God had in store for Weston-Super-Mare.

I knew we were in the right place. There were so many drug rehabs in Weston and people suffering from serious addictions. I was excited to see how God was going to use us. Given my past, I would be here to help the broken, the wounded, and those seeking to break free from their addictions.

The church had a cafe with a huge indoor bouncy castle. It was a great place to connect with people. Within a few weeks I began to make some good connections. I started a group called Rough Diamonds, which is a mixture of people suffering from heroin and crack addictions, along with a few alcoholics. We would always love on them and ask God to help them break free of their addictions and start their journey to recovery.

God did some amazing miracles amongst them in those

meetings. Each of them had a story to tell as to how and why they turned to drugs to hide the pain. One of the girls I will call "Hannah" was constantly raped by her father and brother when she was a teen. Hannah felt trapped, dirty, and suicidal, and one night she jumped from a high motorway bridge and landed on the road below, hoping to die.

Hannah survived the attempt on her own life, but she broke many bones in her body and crippled her legs. As a result, Hannah spent years in a wheelchair. After years of intense therapy, stretches, and exercises, she eventually walked on crutches, but unfortunately, she turned to heroin and crack cocaine to try and hide the pain and trauma from the past.

Hannah soon became addicted to the drugs and began shooting up many times a day. To pay for her heroin and crack habit, she would prostitute her body from her flat and walk the streets in the red-light district in Bradford City Centre at night on her crutches. She sold her body for the price of a spoon full of heroin to hide the pain of shame and feed the addiction.

As Hannah continued to come to the Rough Diamonds group, through prayer God began to slowly bring inner healing and restoration.

But that's not all God wanted to do in her life. When I heard a Benny Hinn healing crusade was in London, I took Hannah and a few other Rough Diamonds in the church minibus and hit the road to London. All the way, I was praying under my breath that they would all come to know Jesus and receive healing in their bodies.

Finally, after four and a half hours, we landed in London and made it in time for the meeting. As we walked into the main room at London Excel, we saw about four thousand people filling the seats. As we walked in, the tangible presence of God filled the air, and we could sense faith and anticipation.

The meeting started, and after many hymns, Benny and his team began ministering to the people. There was a line queuing up to go on stage to testify to the healing God had done in their bodies. People were being healed of tumours. Blind eyes were being opened. Soon wheelchairs were brought onto the stage as people's legs were being healed.

Hannah was weeping as the ministry team came and prayed for her legs. They prayed for both legs a few times and moved on to pray for others. I could feel the presence and the power of God and believed she was healed in that moment. But she could not get out of the wheelchair.

Hannah wept all the way home on the minibus because she was still going home in her chair. The next morning, as the church doors opened, Hannah came running in without her crutches, jumping up and down and spinning around, shouting, "Look! I am healed! I am healed! God's healed me! He loves me!" We jumped together, praised God, and thanked him for her healing. God continued to bring inner healing to Hannah for many months after gently healing her broken heart.

Our God is always willing and faithful to heal and restore the broken and weary. Many times we saw God shower his love on lost and hurting people. It always blows their minds when they find out God loves and cares for them. Most open their hearts to him and follow him for the rest of their lives.

Chapter 47

Growing Our Family

After Andrea and I tried to conceive for many years, God blessed us, and in our first year in Weston-Super-Mare, Andrea gave birth to our first son, Charlie. It was a day we will never forget, holding him in our arms for the first time and finally seeing his cheeky little smiley face. We were both so thankful that God had given us this precious little boy to love.

The church in Weston-Super-Mare continued to grow, where gangs of kids used to hang out on street corners. We got a football and some refreshments and played a few times with the kids in the long, warm summer evenings. Eventually we invited all of them to church and formed our first youth group. They felt they were often judged by the community, who accused them of mischief and trouble, and wanted to do something about it. So, we asked them what Jesus would do in this situation. The answer was, "He would love them and serve." So that's what we decided to do, love them and serve them.

Over the next few days, I travelled around all the big brand superstores and asked them to donate tools for our community action team. Many generously gave to the project and I came home armed with shovels, rakes, hedge trimmers, paints, varnishes, and even a car jet wash. We fixed a date to start, and with a van full of garden tools and teens, we went around our community on the weekends, transforming houses and gardens. It was a great success. Relationships were restored and new friendships were formed. But the greatest fruit from our effort was that many of the kids began to believe in Jesus. Praise God.

Over the next few weeks, it was awesome to see people coming to church for the first time because their lives had been touched by a random act of kindness.

Over the next few years, the church continued to grow steadily. It was during this time that Andrea became pregnant again with our second baby. We were very excited that Charlie was going to have a brother to play with in just nine months' time. During the next nine months, God began to open more doors to testify to others just how awesome he is. One of the weirdest, but most enjoyable, moments was being invited to speak at an annual magistrates' conference. Many times throughout my life I had stood in the dock in the court room and waited for the judges to give me my prison sentence.

Now God had set up a day where I had the opportunity to testify to sixty magistrates at once as I was invited to speak at their annual conference. As always, I seized the opportunity to tell anyone who would listen about God's love and his amazing transforming grace. I was rewarded with an invitation into the private chambers to join the discussions of future sentencing for violent crimes. I felt so awkward and out of place, yet I knew I was there because God had put me there. How else could a prolific offender who has been institutionalised most of his life be sitting in that room? Only God can do such amazing things. He transforms us from the inside out, and we are never the same again.

Nine months passed so quickly, and Andrea gave birth to our second son, Zechariah Daniel.

God blessed us with another good birth and team Rowan soon became four.

Chapter 48

The Beginnings of Full-Time Ministry

During this year, I began studying to become a fully accredited AOG minister. I had never studied for or sat for an exam in my entire life. I rarely went to school as I hid in derelict warehouses, sniffing glue during school hours, and the children's homes didn't do schooling.

My first module came through. I knew I was dyslexic and had pretty much fried my brain over the years tripping out on LSD and dropping ecstasy at all-night raves. But I held onto God's word that I was a new creation because he had transformed me and renewed my mind. I held onto the verse that said all things were possible if I believed. I opened the module, gave it my best shot, and sent it off to be marked.

A couple of weeks later, I received my reply. I had completely failed to answer any of the questions. I used no punctuation, no structure, and all my quotes were from Wikipedia. Needless to say, it was a disaster.

I made a decision that day not to be discouraged. I knew there was a calling on my life, so I asked God for help. A few weeks later I pulled out my terrible marks from my first module and saw them in a different light. Now I had clearer instructions on what not to do. I began writing again and sent it off. A few weeks later, to my surprise, the list of alterations was shorter, and I think I answered the questions. Over the next three years, the marks improved and began to come back, "Good," "Very Good," and finally "Excellent." With God, all things really are possible.

The big day finally came, and with my wife and two boys, we headed off to Mattersey Hall, the Assemblies of God National Ministry Centre for ordination, along with many others coming into full-time ministry. We are really more than conquerors; there is nothing too hard for God.

After a full day of cheers and tears, we headed back to Weston.

We sensed that our time at Weston-Super-Mare had been a great training ground for us and that God was preparing us to enter a new season and chapter in our lives. That was confirmed when a member of the national leadership team of the Assemblies of God invited us for coffee. It turned out that a pastor was needed in a small Pentecostal church, which was a converted boat shed, in Braunton, North Devon. We were asked to pray about it and get back to them.

The location of this opportunity had God's hand all over it. Just a year before we had stayed in a holiday park about a mile away from the church. In fact, we would have passed this church many times, looking around the village of Braunton. We both laughed as we knew God was on our case.

We decided we would pray separately and see what God would say to us. Afterward we discovered God was saying the same thing to both of us. We knew God was orchestrating everything when we applied for the position, and they asked me to come interview with the team and the elders and arrange a date to preach to the congregation.

After a few more preaching dates and meetings, I was invited to take on the role as pastor. I agreed and we soon moved to Braunton for another adventure with God.

The church at Braunton showered us with love. It was mainly an older congregation with no young families. For a few months we settled in and didn't make any changes until we had a clear vision from God.

Chapter 49
Pastoring My First Church

In the first year we renovated the church, changed the name, and invited the community to come to our service. Andrea started a toddler group, which was a great success. It was so good to see children running around, laughing and screaming. We ran a variety of courses, helping people explore God and meet the community's needs.

Families soon began to attend our service and midweek courses. We soon realised Braunton was surrounded by five beaches and was the last stop to pick up anything needed for the beach. Braunton has a large surfing and skateboarding community as most of the community were surfers. It wasn't long before I bought a surfboard and hit the sea.

After a couple of weeks of getting into the sea, through patience, persistence, and watching others, I finally caught my first wave, which was amazing. I soon began making friends in the surfing community, and some of these new friends made it to church, which was awesome. We joined Christian surfers. We built skateparks in car parks near the beach with live music and BBQs. After a surf competition the gospel would be preached from the speaking platform before the trophies were given out. It's always a thrill to see people open their hearts to receive Jesus into their lives.

The church continued to grow as our aim was to make it fun and to enjoy the journey of life together, so we had plenty of church BBQs, surfing, and salsa dance classes in the church hall while still preaching the gospel and making disciples. After a few years, it became clear that we would need a bigger church. We called a meeting to gather the elders and trustees. Both Andrea and I knew God had spoken to us, but we still wondered how the elders and trustees would respond since we had been there only a couple of years.

I felt confident that God had given me a strategy to move the church forward gently. So, I presented the plan to the elders and trustees, and to my amazement, all were in total agreement and praised God.

Even though Braunton is the biggest village in the UK, there was still nowhere we could move to allow the church to grow. So, once again, we asked God for his direction, and he showed us it was time to move the church five miles out of the village to the nearest town, which is Barnstaple. In fact, God showed Andrea that we were going to cross a river to where he wanted us to be—Barnstaple was across the bridge with the river underneath.

In our presentation, when we spoke about moving the church to Barnstaple, some smiled and recounted a specific time seven or eight years previously when it was prophesied the church would move to Barnstaple to grow.

Our strategy was to hire a school hall and some classrooms in Barnstaple once a month. To get people out of their comfort zones and to show them that our plan would work, we began to meet one Sunday a month. Then, after six months, we would meet there every Sunday. Once we committed to meeting every Sunday, we started posting invitations to the community, and the community slowly began to come and check us out.

The months rolled on quickly, and we felt it was time to sell the church in Braunton. God provided a buyer, a local businessman, who bought it for an amount above the asking price, which doesn't happen every day. Again, we thanked and praised God as we knew he was leading and guiding us.

We banked the money and focussed on reaching the town and community in Barnstaple. We began to run regular Alpha courses and weekly connect groups. We focussed our Sunday morning services on worship, evangelism, and missions. We always had an extended time of worship in the presence of God and preached the gospel. Then we gave time for people to respond to the gospel and open their hearts to Jesus. We would often meet at the beach after a service, put up the church flags, and hear the testimonies of those about to be baptized in the sea, which of course was followed by a surf and BBQ.

Chapter 50

My Own Miraculous Healing

During this amazing season of church growth, people were making commitments, being baptized, and getting healed out of the blue. One bright hot summer day, I found myself being rushed to hospital for life-saving surgery.

It was a hot summer day at the school's annual sports day. All the parents and children met on the fields together. The parents would bring picnics and ice cream, and burger vans were in the park with nice music playing. Each class would be given a team name and parents would follow their children around all the challenges and cheer on their children.

At the end of all the obstacles, for fun the children would line up on either side of the running track and cheer on the parents in a race. Now I must admit I am competitive, and I could see my boys lining up to cheer on their dad. Just as we were lining up to race, the headmaster brought out seven space hoppers for us to race on.

I sat on my space hopper and waited for the starter pistol. BOOM! And we are off. I gave my absolute everything in the race but didn't make it first to line.

A few minutes later, after the race, the scores were announced, and the children received their class trophies. Then it was picnic time.

All of a sudden, I felt I was going to collapse. I put on a brave face and asked someone to watch my boys. I stumbled home and managed a quick call to my wife at work before collapsing in our home. My wife asked someone to check to see if I was ok. I was on the floor. An ambulance was called, and I was rushed to hospital.

After a few tests and some oxygen and x-rays, I was rushed into another ambulance and taken to the city hospital. My brain was bleeding, and I had and haemorrhage. My wife was called and told to come quickly if she wanted to see me. I didn't know at the time, but no one thought I was going to survive.

My wife quickly informed the prayer teams to pray urgently. I survived the night, and the next day, God gave a friend a picture of me to give to Andrea. The picture was of her walking down the hospital hall toward my room, with a huge angel walking behind her. I believe it was a healing angel coming to minister to me in Jesus' name.

When Andrea came in the room, even through the regular doses of morphine I could sense the presence of God. When she began to pray, she kept repeating the same phrase over and over: "God's not finished with you yet. Get up in Jesus' name," and again "God's not finished with you yet. Get up in Jesus' name."

I believe from the very moment she began to pray, God started healing the damage to my brain. A few days later God's healing was evident to all as I miraculously was able get up out of my bed, stand on my feet, and walk out of the hospital. The doctors and nurses were all amazed as were we. We praised God and gave him all the glory.

I was so grateful to God for healing me and keeping me alive that I was more determined than ever to tell the world about Jesus.

Chapter 51

Miracles in Barnstaple

Our hearts are always burning to see revival again in the United Kingdom. We continued to meet in the school faithfully every Sunday. Often in the meetings people would testify that they could feel God's presence and, through prayer, were completely healed of their ailments in Jesus' name. Praise God.

We soon began to equip and encourage small groups to operate in the gifts of the Spirit. We would then hit the streets and marketplaces to pray and split off into twos with a central point to meet a couple of hours later to testify.

During these times we saw God do amazing miracles. People gave their lives to Jesus in the high street. When we prayed in Jesus' name, legs grew out before our eyes, and people were encouraged with words of knowledge and prophecy.

At night we took small teams out with flasks of hot soup for those sleeping in shop doorways and preached Jesus to the young gangs of cold, bored teenagers hanging out in the streets. God moved powerfully in some of their lives, and some opened their hearts to Jesus.

We knew we were in the right place in Barnstaple, so we began praying, fasting, and asking God where the church of the future would be. God spoke to Andrea very clearly and told her it was the old cinema. We did some research and found the old cinema was on the strand built in 1937 by a Jewish businessman. When we went to find it, we discovered it had been converted into a nightclub and had been the main nightclub in Barnstaple for the last twenty years.

The next day, someone had a dream and told us the building we would have in the future would have white pillars at the front. Sure enough the nightclub had huge white pillars at the front. We were excited. This place was enormous, but God had put a huge vision in our hearts.

We would often meet in front of that building to pray. As we walked around praying, people stuck scriptures in the cracks of the walls. Others had communion prayer groups that would meet outside the building to repent for Barnstaple's connection with the slave trade in the 1800s and 1900s. One evening God led our local house of prayer to pour some communion down the building drains. They were obedient to God and did exactly what he asked them to do.

Chapter 52

A God-Given Vision for a New Community

A whole year went by, and nothing seemed to be moving with regards to the building, but we were confident that God would let us know what to do when the time was right. One Sunday we had a friend, a pastor from Cambridge, who we invited to come to Devon to take some sessions on Saturday and speak to our church on Sunday morning. He knew nothing of our plans, and at the end of his sermon prophesied that God had been preparing us and that he was about to release a place for us.

A few weeks later I walked past the building as usual to pray and saw the for-sale sign hanging over the front door. I quickly rang and made an enquiry. Apparently because it was an iconic building on the strand, there was lots of interest and it would be going to auction. I noted the date and time of the auction.

Excited, I quickly arranged a meeting to pray and to plan our way forward. We were in no doubt through the crumb trail of dreams, pictures, and prophetic words that God was about to release this building to us. But we realised we had only a small amount of money compared to the asking price

The agent said there was lots of interest and the auction was full, so we got a prayer team together and prayed that God would scatter the buyers in all directions, and that's exactly what happened. The next day I made the call to enquire about the auction and was told it was cancelled due to major issues with an old title deed, and people had lost interest in the building. The only ones left who were interested were us, so we made an offer, which was accepted, and a few weeks later we were picking up the keys.

The building inside was an absolute wreck with leaking roofs and sealed up asbestos rooms. To the natural eye, it seemed crazy that anyone would take on such a huge project with zero money in the bank. But we serve a supernatural God who had given us a clear vision.

As your reading this, we still need well over a million pounds to make this a great place for the community. We don't know how, but we absolutely believe God will supply everything we need. Our vision is to transform it into a community hub, a place in the community for the community. We want to have indoor skatepark facilities with qualified instructors to teach people, especially those suffering from mental health anxieties and depression, to surf and skate.

We also want to offer courses to help people break free from addictions, manage money better, have more successful marriages, acquire better life skills...anything that will help meet our community's needs. It will be a place where:

- People can find God, connect with others, and discover their God-given purpose.
- The lost, broken, and weary can find hope, help, and healing in Jesus' name.
- People will be equipped and encouraged to live supernatural natural lives.
- People will go to the nations to preach the good news that Jesus is alive.

Every time people come for a look around the building, nine out of ten stop on the doorstep, look me in the eye, and tell me "This is a big project."

Every time, I respond with the same answer, "You're right; it's a big job, but I serve a big God, and he will provide."

Chapter 53

Jesus Can Change Your Life Today

Today I woke up in my own bed, kissed my wife, had breakfast with my children, and thanked God for his faithfulness.

Today I thanked God that he planned me for a purpose.

As I bring this book to a close, I want to encourage you and remind you again of the first story I ever read in the Bible in Mark 5. This story has a massive impact on my life.

It is, of course, the story of the demon-possessed man who was bound with a chain and left abandoned in the cemetery on the edge of town. While he was there alone, he cried out for help and tried to take his own life. The Bible says he began to cut himself with sharp stones. He felt alone, rejected, and abandoned.

Somebody heard those cries for help and crossed the sea by boat to get to him. It was, of course, Jesus. When Jesus saw the bleeding, chained man in the cemetery, he cast out the demons and healed the man.

Just one encounter with Jesus changed his life forever, and he went back healed and whole into the towns, amongst the people who had chained him, and told everyone about a living, loving God, who delivered him and set him free. When they saw him walking back into the towns, The Bible says, "and all were amazed." Why? Because he was no longer the same. One encounter with Jesus changed his life forever.

One encounter with JESUS changes everything. There were many times in my own life I felt just like this man. I was out of control, running wild, and causing chaos everywhere I went. But the moment I heard the truth about God's love and grace and encountered Jesus, my life was completely changed, and I was totally set free. I have been healed, restored, and totally transformed from the inside out.

The greatest news of all is the moment I asked Jesus to come into my life. I now get to encounter him every moment of every day, and when I take my final breath in this world, I will see him face to face. Hallelujah!

Maybe you're reading this today and you've felt rejected, abandoned, and alone in life. Maybe you're living a life trapped in chaos and addictions and you don't see any point to life. Maybe you've had a great upbringing and you're doing well, but you don't feel fulfilled. You know something's missing and feel there's got to be more to life.

The answer is, and always was, Jesus. Jesus is the missing piece in your life. Jesus can break the power of any addiction and bring peace to the chaos.

We have all been created to connect with God, to walk with him and talk with him daily. God is love. He loved us all so much that he sent his only Son to die upon the cross for the sins of the world and rose again after three days from the grave in victory.

Why would God do that? Why would Jesus be willing to go through that? Because he loves you and wants to set you free from the weight of your sin right now and give you a new start and a clean slate. Right now, through praying a simple prayer right from the heart, you can ask Jesus into your life.

Romans 10:13 says, "Whoever calls upon the name of the Lord shall be saved."

Here's a prayer you can pray with right now to receive Jesus into your heart and life. Let's pray.

> *"Dear Lord Jesus,*
> *I know I am a sinner, and I ask for your forgiveness.*
> *I believe you died and rose again from the dead.*
> *I trust and follow you as my Lord and Saviour.*
> *Guide my life and help me to do your will.*
> *In Jesus' name, Amen."*

If you have just prayed that prayer with me, welcome brother and sister to the family of the kingdom of God. The Bible tells us when one person gives their life to Jesus, the angels in heaven rejoice and party.

One day you will see Jesus face to face and join the party. But right now, I say to you the same words Jesus said to the demon-possessed man who was healed that day in the cemetery.

Mark 5:16: "Go home to your friends and tell them what great things the Lord had done for you and how he has had compassion on you."

I believe as you go, just as the man did in this passage, people will marvel as they will see the power of God really does transform lives.

Be faithful and fruitful in all you do in Jesus' name. God bless you.

If you would like to contact Mark Rowan, reach him at:

markrowanccc@gmail.com

www.hubonthestrand.co.uk

www.ingramcontent.com/pod-product-compliance
Lightning Source LLC
LaVergne TN
LVHW021705060526
838200LV00050B/2515